MANAGING PROFESSIONAL DEVELOPMENT IN SCHOOLS

The importance of professional development for teachers cannot be overstated. In recent years there has been much debate on how to raise standards in schools, and it is now recognised by theorists, policy makers and practitioners that the professional development of teachers is an important factor in this context.

For professional development co-ordinators and senior management, knowledge and understanding of human resource management theories and of the nature of professional development roles will provide a framework for practice.

The book includes chapters on:

- managing professional development in a human resources context
- government National Standards for Teachers
- initial teacher training
- the school development plan
- appraisal
- middle management
- leadership skills

It will be of interest to co-ordinators of professional development in schools and across local education authorities, and to anyone who is part of a school's senior management team.

Sonia Blandford is deputy-head of the School of Education at Oxford Brookes University and is also the author of *Managing Discipline in Schools*.

EDUCATIONAL MANAGEMENT SERIES
Series editors: Sonia Blandford and John Welton

Recent titles in this series include:

MANAGING DISCIPLINE IN SCHOOLS

Sonia Blandford

THE PRIMARY SCHOOL IN CHANGING TIMES: THE AUSTRALIAN EXPERIENCE

Edited by Tony Townsend

SCHOOL CHOICE AND COMPETITION: MARKETS IN THE PUBLIC INTEREST

Philip Woods, Carl Bagley and Ron Glatter

CHOICE AND DIVERSITY IN SCHOOLING: PERSPECTIVES AND PROSPECTS

Edited by Ron Glatter, Philip Woods and Carl Bagley

MANAGING INFORMATION TECHNOLOGY IN SCHOOLS

Roger Crawford

CONTINUING PROFESSIONAL DEVELOPMENT

Anna Craft

SUCCESS AGAINST THE ODDS

The National Commission on Education

MANAGING SPECIAL NEEDS IN THE PRIMARY SCHOOL

Joan Dean

THE SKILLS OF PRIMARY SCHOOL MANAGEMENT

Les Bell and Chris Rhodes

EDUCATION FOR THE TWENTY-FIRST CENTURY

Hedley Beare and Richard Slaughter

MAKING GOOD SCHOOLS

Edited by Robert Bollen, Bert Creemers, David Hopkins, Louise Stoll and Nijs Lagerweij

INNOVATIVE SCHOOL PRINCIPLES AND RESTRUCTURING

Clive Dimmock and Tom O'Donoghue

THE SELF-MONITORING PRIMARY SCHOOL

Edited by Pearl White and Cyril Poster

MANAGING RESOURCES FOR SCHOOL IMPROVEMENT

Hywel Thomas and Jane Martin

SCHOOLS AT THE CENTRE: A STUDY OF DECENTRALISATION

Alison Bullock and Hywel Thomas

DEVELOPING EFFECTIVE SCHOOL MANAGEMENT

Jack Dunham

MEETING THE CHALLENGES OF PRIMARY SCHOOLING

Edited by Lloyd Logan and Judyth Sachs

RESTRUCTURING AND QUALITY IN TOMORROW'S SCHOOLS

Edited by Tony Townsend

THE ETHICAL SCHOOL

Felicity Haynes

IMPROVING THE PRIMARY SCHOOL

Joan Dean

RESTRUCTURING: THE KEY TO EFFECTIVE SCHOOL MANAGEMENT

Cyril Poster

Edited by Sonia Blandford and John Welton

MANAGING PROFESSIONAL DEVELOPMENT IN SCHOOLS

Sonia Blandford

Foreword by John Welton

London and New York

First published 2000
by Routledge
11 New Fetter Lane, London EC4P 4EE

Simultaneously published in the USA and Canada
by Routledge
29 West 35th Street, New York, NY 10001

Routledge is an imprint of the Taylor & Francis Group

© 2000 Sonia Blandford

Typeset in Garamond by Taylor & Francis Books Ltd
Printed and bound in Great Britain by St Edmundsbury Press, St
Edmundsbury, Suffolk

British Library Cataloguing in Publication Data
A catalogue record for this book is available from the British Library

Library of Congress Cataloguing in Publication Data
Blandford, Sonia.
Managing professional development in schools / Sonia Blandford.
p. cm. – (Educational management series.
Includes bibliographical references (p.) and index.
1. Teachers–In-service training–Great Britain–Administration.
I. Title. II. Series.
LB1731.B57   2000   99–41939
370' .71'55–dc21   CIP

ISBN 0–415–19759–7

TO CHARLIE AND BETHANY

CONTENTS

CONTENTS

ILLUSTRATIONS

FIGURES

FOREWORD

There is an old story about the headteacher who when asked how many people worked in his school, always replied in terms of numbers of teaching and support staff, completely forgetting the children. Sonia Blandford's book challenges us to discard a similar set of blinkers and consider how many people 'learn' in a school? Sonia demonstrates the way in which the concept of 'learning organisation' applies to schools. Just as the various domains of learning constitute the 'work' of school students, professional 'learning' is an intrinsic part of the work of teachers. Learning, is a fundamental component of the work of any profession, and for teachers, this does not only include the requirement to keep their academic knowledge up-to-date. Teachers need to regularly update their understanding of the ways in which children and adults learn, as well as learn from new knowledge about effective ways of teaching, and school organisation. Teachers also need to maintain their wider knowledge of trends outside schools including the policy and regulatory framework for education.

Sonia has written a book which seeks to be a practical handbook for the busy teacher and administrator, as well as challenging assumptions by drawing together dimensions of school organisation and management from different milieus. The concepts and practices fundamental to Total Quality Management and the Investor in People (IIP) Standard are increasingly familiar within schools and colleges. Fundamental to the success of both TQM and IIP is change that is based on local initiative for a change in organisational culture, rather than external coercion.

The jury is out on how far nearly two decades of political pressure and admonition can change the quality of schools for the better. In the meantime, it seems curious that during a period when the conventional wisdom of successive national governments has been that organisations are most effective when released from central control, that theory has been turned on its head when applied to education. This book challenges all the practitioners, managers, local education authorities, higher education institutions, the Teacher Training Agency and politicians to understand how change occurs from the bottom up by developing the school as a learning community.

Professor John Welton
Oxford Brookes University

PREFACE

The purpose of this book is to provide guidance for practitioners – managers and teachers – on how to manage the professional development function in schools. Placed within the context of total quality management, lifelong learning initiatives, the emerging national standards for teachers and more established inservice training and education programmes, this book will both inform and direct readers, leading them to an understanding of the function of professional development and its impact on policy, procedures and practice in schools.

The emphasis is on the management of professional development in schools, through which teachers can develop personally and professionally, thus contributing to the development of a learning organisation in which the emphasis is on quality and learning.

If professional development is to be effective, schools will have to develop a culture of learning for all members of their communities. A school will have to work in partnership with the government, the Teacher Training Agency (TTA), the teachers' unions, the local education authority (LEA), its governors and the parents of its pupils to create a learning organisation in which every person is valued. A learning school is an organisation moving forward, and at the centre of its evolving community is education.

As this book addresses a broad issue that affects all levels of the teaching profession, it is written for

- primary and secondary school practitioners – trainee teachers, teachers, middle and senior managers, headteachers, returners to the profession;
- school governors;
- educators of teachers – higher education institutions;
- consultants – short-courses leaders, National Professional Qualification for Headship trainers;
- the Teacher Training Agency – policy makers, trainers and centre managers;
- LEAs – policy makers and advisors.

The book is presented in three parts: Part I focuses on the principles and practice of managing professional development in schools, total quality management, culture, and the Investor in People (IIP) standard. Part II introduces current government policies and initiatives on professional development in schools, encompassing the national standards for teachers, the Advanced Skills Teacher grade, and evaluations of the National Professional Qualification for Headship, Headteacher Leadership and Management Programme and the Leadership Programme for Serving Headteachers. Part III provides guidance to managers and individual teachers on school-based professional development. Beginning with a consideration of school development plans, the focus moves on to staff appraisal, middle management, managing professional development as a resource, and the management of whole-school inservice education and training for teachers. The book concludes with a deliberation on the way forward for the management of professional development in schools.

The focus of this book is management of the professional development of teachers; the developmental needs of support staff and governors are not covered. The author acknowledges the importance of these learning community members, however, and directs the reader to works by John Coe (1999 Oxford Brookes University), for support staff, and Peter Earley (1999 Institute of Education, University of London), for governors.

The challenge to practitioners, managers, LEAs, HEIs, the TTA and the government is how to draw together the good practice that already exists in schools with more recent initiatives. This book addresses that challenge by weaving together the three strands of professional development: schools as learning organisations; the national standards for teachers and the standards fund; and school and individual development plans and activities.

ACKNOWLEDGEMENTS

This book would not have been written without the expertise, encouragement and time given by researchers and practitioners. I express my thanks to Christopher Hart, head of English, Little Heath School, Berkshire; Brenda Williams, former first school deputy headteacher; Dawn Newstead, head of drama, Devizes School, Wiltshire; Judith Rawlings, primary practitioner; John Welton, professor of education, Oxford Brookes University; Linet Arthur, senior lecturer in education management, Oxford Brookes University; Irene Scott, course leader for the Secondary Postgraduate Certificate in Education (PGCE), Oxford Brookes University.

Special thanks go to Rachel Soper, Charlie Eldridge, John Wood and Paul Trembling for their contributions to the production of this book.

Finally, I pay tribute to the patience and support of my husband Charlie Eldridge.

The author and publisher wish to thank the copyright holders for permission to reproduce figures and extracts in this book. Acknowledgements for figures are made with the captions. Crown copyright is reproduced with the permission of the Controller of Her Majesty's Stationery Office. Text relating to the Department for Education and Employment Green Paper and Technical Paper appears on pages: 63, 77, 79, 91, 92, 93, 94, 101–2, 105, 109, 112, 117, 118, 143, 144, 158, 172, 175, 199, 200, 201 and 202. Every effort has been made to obtain permission to reproduce copyright material. If any proper acknowledgement has not been made, we would invite copyright holders to inform us of the oversight.

ABBREVIATIONS

ACAS	Advisory Conciliation and Arbitration Service
AST	Advanced Skills Teacher
BA (QTS)	Bachelor of Education (Qualified Teachers Status)
BEd	Bachelor of Education
BITC	Business in the Community
CBI	Confederation of British Industry
CEO	chief education officer
CEP	Career Entry Profile
CPD	continuing professional development
DDP	department development plan
DES	Department of Education and Science
DfEE	Department for Education and Employment
EdD	Doctor of Education
EDP	educational development plan
EMIE	Education Management Information Exchange
ERA	Education Reform Act
ESRC	Economic and Social Research Council
GCSE	General Certificate of Secondary Education
GEST	Grants for Education Support and Training
GTC	General Teaching Council
HEADLAMP	Headteacher Leadership And Management Programme
HEI	higher education institution
HEFCE	Higher Education Funding Council for England
HRM	human resource management
ICT	information, communication and technology
IIP	Investors in People
INSET	Inservice Education for Teachers
IPM	Institute of Personnel Management
IT	information technology
ITT(E)	initial teacher training (education)
LEA	local education authority
LMS	local management of schools

MA	Master of Arts
NAHT	National Association of Head Teachers
NASSP	National Association of Secondary School Principals
NCE	National Commission on Education
NDCEMP	National Development Centre for Education Management and Policy
NEAC	National Educational Assessment Centre
NFER	National Foundation for Education Research
NPBEA	National Policy Board for Education Administration
NPQH	National Professional Qualification for Headteachers
NPQSENCO	National Professional Qualification for Special Educational Needs' Co-ordinators
NPQSH	National Professional Qualification for Serving Headteachers
NPQSL	National Professional Qualification for Subject Leaders
NQT	newly qualified teacher
NTTF	National Training Task Force
NUT	National Union of Teachers
NVQ	National Vocational Qualification
OfSTED	Office for Standards in Education
PDP	Professional Development Profile
PTD	professional training days
PGCE	Post Graduate Certificate in Education
PhD	Doctor of Philosophy
QTS	Qualified Teacher Status
SCITT	school-centred initial teacher training
SDP	school development plan
SEN	special educational needs
SENCO	special educational needs co-ordinator
SHA	Secondary Headteachers' Association
SMTF	School Management Task Force
SRB	single regeneration budget
TEC	Training and Enterprise Council
TES	*Times Educational Supplement*
TQM	total quality management
TTA	Teacher Training Agency
UCET	Universities' Council for the Education of Teachers

Part I

THE SCHOOL AS
A LEARNING
ORGANISATION

This section introduces the principles that inform the management of professional development within schools as learning organisations.

Chapter 1 introduces the management of professional development in schools, focusing on the school as a learning organisation, and defines the emerging principles. Also introduced here is the role of the school professional development co-ordinator.

Chapter 2 examines human resource management theories and defines total quality management as the underlying principle for the management of professional development within a learning organisation.

Chapter 3 traces the origins of the Investor in People standard, a government initiative that promotes professional development in organisations. A case study of a secondary school is presented as a means of determining the place of IIP within the context of schools as learning organisations.

INTRODUCTION

Management theory, on first reading, can appear to be distanced from management practice. For professional development co-ordinators and senior management, knowledge and understanding of the nature of professional development roles and human resource management theories provide the framework for practice. The theoretical underpinning of workplace functions, which is further evidenced by the implementation of theory in practice, will provide practitioners with the tools with which to reflect on and evaluate the quality of teaching and learning in their schools.

The importance of professional development for teachers cannot be overstated. In recent years there has been much debate on how to raise standards in schools, and the importance of the professional development of teachers for the raising of standards is now recognised by theorists, policy-makers and practitioners. An understanding of the role of the professional development co-ordinator is therefore required. Rawlings has helped to clarify this area of school management, and she presents (1997) an evidence-based summary of the practical implementations of managing professional development in schools. Bolam's views (1993) on the nature of professional development are illuminating, serving to provide co-ordinators with a framework of the range of developmental opportunities available for practitioners. This understanding of professional development when linked with notions of adult learning (Honey and Mumford 1986) leads to the conclusion that the management of professional development in schools would be more effective if understood within the context of a human resource management (HRM) theory in contrast to the bureaucratic approach adopted by many LEAs and schools. The adoption of HRM principles by schools, discussed in Chapter 3, will be shown to be empowering. HRM in its different forms is aimed at developing rather than directing people.

Furthermore, the holistic approach of Total Quality Management (TQM) enables practitioners to view practice from a theoretical perspective. The introduction of the IIP standard in a secondary school provides a case-study analysis of TQM in practice, with the outcome overall proving to be a positive one. Such evidence-based examples are useful points of reference for managers and teachers.

The relationship between theory, research and practice in education is reflected in the professional development of practitioners. As will be shown in Part I, the knowledge and understanding of theory can, and will, develop the skills and abilities of practitioners.

1

MANAGING PROFESSIONAL DEVELOPMENT IN SCHOOLS

INTRODUCTION

The expertise and experience of its academic and administrative staff are a school's most valuable resource, and for all teachers learning and development are central to professional practice. Throughout the 1980s and 1990s, whole-school in-service education and training for teachers were considered by the government to be a suitable means by which to implement professional development for teachers and, more specifically, change. Since 1985, five days per academic year (so-called 'Baker days') have been allocated in all schools for staff development. After almost a decade, the government began to voice its recognition that the impact on practice of such training provision had been limited (TTA 1994) and that this was due, in part, to ineffective management by schools of the professional development of their teachers.

The government has addressed this issue by introducing a range of initiatives designed to improve the management of professional development. The challenge facing schools, and to a lesser extent the government, is how to manage these new initiatives alongside existing developmental activities. The first step in addressing this challenge is to establish just what opportunities are available for teachers.

The range of available professional development initiatives that will be discussed in this book is outlined in Table 1.1.

The management of teachers' professional development encompasses many issues in addition to knowing what is available. The culture of *the learning organisation* and the diversity of adult learning styles are core issues to be addressed in this book, as also are the nature and function of professional development. These themes are discussed within the framework of whole-school development planning, starting with professional development.

Table 1.1   A guide to coverage

Topic	Chapter
Standards Fund (LEA)	1
Total quality management/Investors in People	2, 3
National standards for teachers	4–7
Unions/diocese	5–7
Advanced Skills Teachers award	6
HE courses	6
School development	8
Appraisal	9
Management development	10
In-school training	11
Performance management	12

PROFESSIONAL DEVELOPMENT

Professional development performs four major functions within a school. It serves to

1   enhance individual performance;
2   rectify ineffective practice;
3   establish the groundwork for the implementation of policy;
4   facilitate change.

As such, professional development includes personal development, team development and school development. In addition to developing individual skills, professional development has a wider importance in promoting *shared values* and *equality of opportunity*.

If professional development is to be effective, *resources* (human and financial) must be allocated and directed to meet individual and school targets. *Appraisal* and *inspection* should also be seen as integral to the planning of professional development.

The effective management of professional development depends on individual enthusiasm, not compulsion, and on individuals prepared to take action in addressing their own professional needs. In a learning organisation staff will recognise for themselves the importance of keeping up-to-date, maintaining good practice and networking with others. *Structures and systems* have to be in place for the review and development of each member of the learning organisation. Effective communication is essential if all staff are to benefit from developmental opportunities.

In practice, the responsibility for developing staff is *shared*. The school as a whole has a responsibility to develop policies and provide resources for staff development. Professional development is not to be seen as something tagged-on to the other day-to-day functions of teachers: rather, it should be central to the process of *strategic development planning* which provides staff with in-house opportunities and guidance on new initiatives. Professional development should be considered integral to the management of innovation, change and reform.

A school which is a learning organisation will be able to make continuous improvements whilst adapting to change in the external environment. This is of particular importance in view of the requirements of the government's new initiatives and changed funding arrangements, and their impact on the practice of professional development in schools. Those involved in the management of schools need to be aware of the internal and external parameters within which they work: confusion in these respects will lead to frustration and conflict.

The Purpose of Professional Development

The purpose of professional development can be summarised as the acquisition or extension of the knowledge, understanding, skills and abilities that will enable individual teachers and the schools—learning organisations in which they work to

- develop and adapt their range of practice;
- reflect on their experience, research and practice in order to meet pupil needs, collectively and individually;
- contribute to the professional life of the school, and as a practitioner interact with the school community and external agencies;
- keep in touch with current educational thinking in order to maintain and develop good practice;
- give critical consideration to educational policy, in particular how to raise standards;
- widen their understanding of society, in particular of information and communication technology (ICT).

An educational institution's approach to professional development will depend on whether it views employees as a resource or a cost—commodity, its view of adults as lifelong learners, its educational goals and preferred methods for achieving them. These issues are discussed in more detail in Chapter 2. Ultimately, in each school, the aim of professional development is to improve practice in the classroom.

Management Teams

In their early professional years individual teachers, assisted and guided by the management teams responsible for their employment and the support of their development, should seek to develop abilities in respect of

- recognising the diverse talents and capabilities of their individual pupils;
- identifying and providing for the special learning needs, strengths and weaknesses of all pupils;
- evaluating, assessing and reporting on their pupils' learning and adjusting their expectations as teachers accordingly;
- providing for the social, moral, spiritual and cultural development of their pupils;
- their own professional knowledge, skills, strategies, techniques, beliefs and values, and personal characteristics such as awareness, imagination and enterprise;
- their working relationships with their teaching and support colleagues, the parents of their pupils, the governors of the school, and members of external agencies;
- their administrative, pastoral and legal responsibilities.

Types of Professional Development

Teachers and support staff will normally associate professional development with In-service Education for Teachers (INSET), defined as 'planned activities practised both within and outside schools primarily to develop the professional knowledge, skills, attitudes and performance of professional staff in schools' (Hall and Oldroyd 1990c). INSET has been a 'catch-all' term encompassing diverse continuing professional development and training opportunities. In practice, the only experience of INSET for the majority of teachers is of the compulsory training days managed by either LEA advisory teams or senior managers in schools. This should change soon, as the government now requires all schools to have a professional development policy that affords a range of opportunities and modes of participation.

The management of professional development will involve consideration of different types of professional development activity (Bolam 1993), including:

Practitioner development	School-based development, self-development, induction, mentoring, observation, job-shadowing and team teaching
Professional education	Award bearing courses managed and taught at higher education institutions (HEIs), focusing on the relationship between educational theory and

practice, and leading to higher education accreditation and professional qualifications

Professional training Conferences, courses and workshops that emphasise practical information and skills, managed and delivered by LEAs, schools' external consultants or trainers from HEIs. Such courses may lead to academic awards or accreditation towards national standards

Professional support Provided by colleagues and managers in fulfilment of contractual conditions of service; e.g. recruitment and selection procedures (including job descriptions), promotion, career development, appraisal, mentoring, team building, redeployment and equality of opportunity.

How each of the above is implemented will depend on the knowledge, skills and abilities of individuals, teams, managers and advisors. Part III offers practical advice on professional development activities for teachers in a learning organisation. The quality of such activities will depend, in turn, on the extent to which a school approximates a learning community with a positive developmental culture.

Policy

The effective school will have a professional development policy which is generated by a team representing the views of staff at all levels. To begin with, the analysis of institutional strategies for development and individual appraisal targets provides the information that will determine the content and direction of the policy. That there is tension between the individual and institutional requirements of staff development is well known, so that when planning a professional development programme it is important to try to find a balance between the needs of the institution and the aspirations of all who work within it. These two elements generally overlap, though initially differences in priorities will have to be accommodated. It is through the management of a detailed planning process that the professional development policy will be able to relate individual needs to school targets.

A professional development programme should encompass provision by LEAs, external agencies, in-school initiatives and, where appropriate, HEIs. Relevant data, such as that on inspection outcomes, will inform senior managers and the professional development co-ordinator of the needs of the school and its teachers in the context of external demands and opportunities. Having decided on the content and direction of the policy document, the next stage is to plan the provision of resources to enable targets to be met. The final part of the policy process is monitoring, evaluating and reviewing activities to ensure that each target has been properly addressed. Any evaluation of practice should provide managers with the information relevant to the development of their organisation.

THE LEARNING ORGANISATION

Learning organisations are created and sustained by learning communities. A learning community is comprised of individuals each of whom, in addition to performing his or her duties, has opportunities for learning. A learning community will formally recognise and value the learning that takes place within and beyond itself. In such a community learning is managed by individuals, their teachers and helpers, team leaders and managers. It is through the recognition of itself as a learning community that a school becomes a learning organisation, and this requires the formal acknowledgement of the right to learn of each member of the organisation. Schools that are learning organisations are centred upon the teaching, support and administrative staff who lead, direct and contribute to its evolution and development. A learning organisation is one that is able to set, plan and meet targets. It is also a reflective organisation, able to identify strengths, weaknesses, opportunities and threats, and professional in the way it manages and develops staff. Crucially, a learning organisation is continually in search of ways in which to improve itself.

In a learning organisation opportunities are provided to learn how to learn. This enables staff to assimilate and respond to new areas of knowledge and to develop the skills required to address issues as they emerge. It is now recognised that central to lifelong learning is the ability of individuals to absorb new information and to encounter new situations (Fryer 1998). This is particularly pertinent to practitioners in the current climate, where professional and career initiatives for teachers and managers require individuals to manage their own learning accounts and to develop their own quality goals.

Within a learning organisation the close relationship between professional and organisational development is reflected in the community's culture. If a school is to become a learning organisation, a culture of learning that encompasses and celebrates the professional and personal development of its staff is required. Such development should be funded and supported through government policies and training initiatives (DfEE 1999a). Further and higher education institutions are also able to support schools: with their combined knowledge and skills they can provide the stimulus required for individual and institutional growth. It is within a learning organisation that professional development will become fully effective.

CULTURE

A good professional development culture is crucial to the creation of a learning organisation, as also is effective implementation of the staff development policy. The management of a professional development culture involves

- the acceptance that professional development continues throughout working life, i.e. lifelong learning;
- establishing, through induction and appraisal, an awareness of the importance of continuous learning;
- providing staff with access to a variety of learning experiences;
- providing expert support and guidance on professional development issues for all staff;
- encouraging reflection and development;
- motivating, valuing and rewarding all staff in the learning community.

These themes are considered in the context of total quality management in Chapters 2 and 3, and are further developed in Chapter 12.

CAREER MANAGEMENT

Those who manage professional development will recognise that teachers' career development is most effectively managed by the individuals them-selves, with guidance and support from management teams. Managers should recognise also that the importance of continuous support in the development of a teacher's career stems from modifications to the role of educational practitioners (see Table 1.2); moreover, the rapid changes to the curriculum and the devolution of management responsibilities from LEAs to schools have led to a shift in management styles affecting schools as organisations:

Table 1.2   Changes to teachers' practice

From	*To*
Fixed roles	Flexible roles
Individual responsibility	Shared responsibility
Autocratic	Collaborative
Control	Release
Power	Empowerment
Managed	Managing

Table 1.2 indicates changes in the roles of managers and practitioners. All teachers now are involved in a range of day-to-day management tasks: teaching, planning and primary learning, and resources; collaboration on clearly defined tasks; monitoring and evaluation. They participate by representation in working groups set up by the senior management team to discuss specific tasks or directives issuing from governing agencies or school policy groups. Such changes will, inevitably, impact on each teacher's career.

As professionals, teachers are enabled to make their own decisions concerning their careers, though, as members of a learning organisation, they will be assisted and guided in their career development. This investment in a teacher's development will be reflected in his or her commitment to teaching.

How this is achieved in practice requires further elaboration. Table 1.3 illustrates the learning organisation's commitment to a teacher's career, beginning with his or her recruitment and selection for a particular post. This leads to appointment, positioning and induction, followed by the process of appraisal and its outcome – targeted training and development. The final component in a career framework is the diversity of options that present themselves at the end of a contract in a school (or indeed the end of a career). Each of these stages is developed in this book.

Table 1.3 reflects the practical importance of human resource management theory, and this is developed in Chapters 2 and 3.

Table 1.3 illuminates also the importance of a collegial approach to the management of professional development, indicating that effective professional development opportunities are the result of collaboration, participation and negotiation. A teacher's career should be viewed as a continuum in which is embedded the right of access to support at any point. Such an approach, wider than simply succession planning for promotion to senior management, requires a detailed analysis of the needs and aspirations of the profession in order to meet them as fully as possible.

The Teacher Training Agency's national standards' framework is the most significant government initiative for professional development since the introduction of 'Baker days' (DES 1985). Figure 1.1 illustrates the stages of a teacher's career in relation to the Teacher Training Agency's *National Standards for Teachers* (1998e), details of which are given in Part II.

The introduction of the *National Standards for Teachers* is the latest in a series of governmental drives to raise standards in schools.

Table 1.3   Aspects of career management and related human resource planning
issues

Career management	Human resource planning
Recruitment	Knowing/influencing the supply of available talent
• Attracting applicants	Use of agencies or search firms
• Defining requirements	Defining staffing needs
• Selection	Defining *bona fide* job requirements
• Induction and orientation	Providing information to recruits
	Validation of selection process
	Shortening the learning curve
	Minimising early turnover
Placement	Defining professional and managerial job requirements and job families/career paths
• Identifying job requirements and career paths	Designing job descriptions
• Inventories and placement systems	Defining the level of employee involvement
• Job posting and bidding	Validation of internal selection procedures
• Fast-track programmes	Managing accelerated career progress for high-potential employees
• Management succession programme	Controlling relocations and minimising their disruptive effects
• Relocations	
Training and development	Enabling employees to do their own career planning effectively
• Individual career planning	Managing raised expectations
• Training needs' analysis	Defining developmental needs
• Programme design and development	Weighing alternative means of meeting needs
• Research and evaluation	Evaluating the costs, benefits and quality of programmes
De-recruitment and alternatives	Policy and philosophy regarding reverse or lateral career steps
• Termination	Policy governing termination and consideration of legality
• Retirement	Devising flexible retirement policies and practices
• Demotion and transfer	

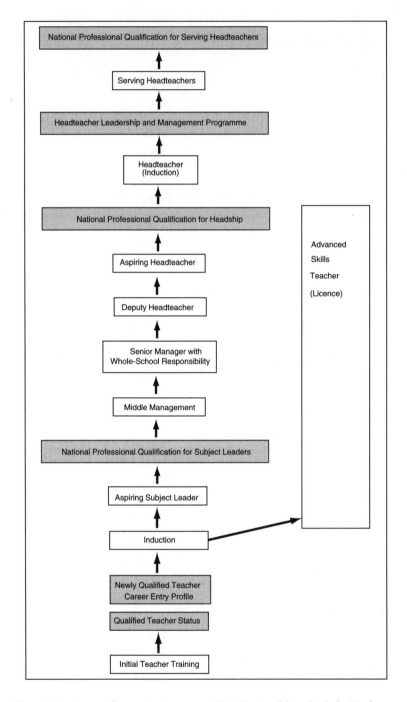

Figure 1.1   Stages of a teacher's career – TTA *National Standards for Teachers*

PROFESSIONAL DEVELOPMENT AND EFFECTIVE SCHOOLS

School governors and managers now have greater responsibility than in previous years for the training and development of the staff in their learning community. Members of an effective school will see themselves as belonging to a learning organisation in which staff are valued. This is confirmed by the last two decades' research into school effectiveness which emphasises the importance of leadership in the management of professional development (see Rutter et al. 1979; Mortimore et al. 1988; DES 1990; Sammons et al. 1995). Research on school improvement carried out during the 1990s (DfEE–OfSTED 1994; Stoll and Fink 1996) continues to promote this theme. In response to this research and to government policy, training and induction opportunities for teachers in England have undergone radical change (Baker 1996; Male 1997) and are currently the focus of the substantial government reforms which are examined in Part II.

It is now understood that professional development is a prerequisite for effective schools (Green 1999). Successful schools do not simply happen; they are successful because people make them so and all such people have a stake in school management. Professional development as an integral component of effective schools will contribute to the creation of a learning environment that has high reinforcement of good practice. In order to be effective, managers and teachers will need to engage in professional development. A fundamental principle of the learning organisation and the focus of a good school is effective learning; consequently, it is the task of management to create the conditions which enable teachers and pupils to achieve effective learning. Further, effective schools will need to increase the capability of school management to undertake this task.

Effective managers will assist staff in their development by

- providing role models of good practice and attitude;
- arranging specific guidance/training;
- encouraging reflection;
- sensitive delegation;
- promoting developmental initiatives;
- providing information and developmental opportunities as they arise.

An effective manager will aim to improve the qualities of existing staff in order to achieve school targets. Professional development also has a wider importance in the context of effective schools of promoting shared values, implementing change and promoting equality of opportunity.

An effective professional development programme is also a means of contributing to and monitoring progress. Ultimately, the time committed to the professional development of teachers will be reflected in pupil learning outcomes. This is important, as professional development will often remove teachers from their classrooms. The question needs to be asked: is this an effective use of a teacher's time? If the outcome is to enhance and improve practitioner skills, this will do much to develop purposeful and focused teaching. Professional development in effective schools will

- emphasise individuals' development within the organisational context;
- increase the number of individuals undergoing staff development;
- relate professional development to the context of the school and integrate it with other developmental initiatives;
- relate professional development to both individual and school needs;
- provide professional development opportunities through collaboration, participation and negotiation.

CO-ORDINATING PROFESSIONAL DEVELOPMENT

Given the complexity of the initiatives and opportunities available, practitioners require guidance on the kind of provision likely to assist them in the development of their professional practice. Schools currently allocate the management of professional development programmes and funds either to a deputy headteacher (or aspiring deputy headteacher) or to a middle manager (Rawlings 1997). In the majority of primary schools, it is the responsibility of an already over-committed headteacher. Evidence from a review of OfSTED reports (Levacic and Glover 1995) suggests that those responsible for planning professional development in schools should follow a planning approach, linking priorities for expenditure more closely to school aims.

The role of the staff development co-ordinator is to establish the development needs of individuals and to have the knowledge and ability actively to promote and support their development within the overall developmental aims of the institution (Rawlings 1997). In order to do this, the staff development co-ordinator must have knowledge about, and involvement with, many areas of school life, including:

- school development planning
- OfSTED preparation and follow-up
- staff development planning
- staff appraisal
- management of the standards' budget
- knowledge of whole-school budgetary planning
- knowledge of bids and funding procedures
- financial management
- mentoring staff and students

- induction of new staff and newly qualified teachers (NQTs)
- co-ordinating INSET.

This involvement will allow the co-ordinator to have an overview of the developmental needs of the school as a whole and of the individuals within it. The co-ordinator can then plan for appropriate development, prioritising needs. The co-ordinator will need to understand fully the criteria required by the Standards Fund (Chapter 4) in order to match the development needs of individuals to available finances and to be able to advise staff accordingly. She or he will need an understanding of financial management, including making forecasts and bids, administering the budget and evaluating effectiveness (Blandford 1997b).

The professional development co-ordinator in each school is responsible for integrating the management of internal and external activities. In practice, the effectiveness of the co-ordinator's work will be dependent on the management of

- information – available for all staff concerning continuing professional development (CPD) programmes, INSET, the Standards Fund, and the national standards for teachers;
- planning – collaboration between multi-agencies in consultation with their teams;
- evaluation – of all courses, teachers' needs in relation to pupils' and the school's needs;
- resources – utilising expertise within the school and of LEAs, external agencies, HEIs, the Teacher Training Agency and other consultants;
- networking – facilitating consultation between management and teams and INSET providers;
- providers of training and consultancy expertise in order to assess their potential to give value for money.

To appreciate the developmental needs of both institution and individuals, the co-ordinator requires considerable knowledge and expertise, and a clear vision for the future. Hall and Oldroyd (1990c) identified eight roles applicable to the position of staff development co-ordinator:

- counsellor
- motivator
- innovator
- mentor
- monitor
- evaluator
- administrator
- facilitator

The co-ordinator must be effective also as a manager and a leader, roles requiring highly developed professional skills, including those of

- gauging where the institution is and where it is going in the future;
- ascertaining the undisclosed needs of individual staff;
- understanding what motivates individual staff;
- managing budgets and other aspects of finance;
- influencing senior management on appropriate courses of action;
- listening and communicating;
- dealing with people: accessibility and approachability are vital.

Ideally, the co-ordinator will have received training for these functions prior to taking on the role; in reality, however, they are found frequently to have several developmental needs. Rawlings (1997) found that the most pressing need identified by co-ordinators themselves was for training in financial and budgetary management, especially the integration of budgetary and developmental planning. Other areas of training need identified were evaluation skills and techniques, collating or formulating the SDP, time-management skills and skills relating to the roles of counsellor, motivator and mentor.

The Key Tasks of the Staff Development Co-ordinator

The role of the school's staff development co-ordinator will include some or all of the following functions:

- overseeing the cycle of staff development and keeping it on course;
- facilitating and supporting the staff development group and, where necessary, liaising between the group and the headteacher (if the headteacher is not a member of the group);
- communicating information to staff;
- managing staff development and encouraging the adoption of appropriate management techniques and attitudes;
- assisting in the identification and prioritising of needs;
- arranging and, where necessary, administering interviews, questionnaires and other paperwork;
- designing or helping others to design courses, and organising and running school-based courses;
- liaising with the LEA staff development advisers, the INSET co-ordinator, the cluster providers and representing the school at meetings with outside agencies;
- ensuring that the school derives maximum benefit from every course by stimulating and overseeing the dissemination of information and by 'cascading';

- designing and implementing the evaluation of staff development and INSET;
- maintaining records of courses attended and staff expertise thereby acquired for use in future courses or 'self-help' groups.

Adey and Jones (1997) identified several concerns regarding staff or professional development co-ordinators' ability to manage professional development. These relate primarily to the role's lack of recognised status, which frequently results in only partial involvement of the co-ordinator in the process of planning and budgetary strategy. Lack of status for the role is often reflected in the insufficient time allocated to co-ordinators for effective performance. Without status, communication is difficult. Professional development co-ordinators often find that they lack information following appraisal; they may also experience a lack of understanding of the co-ordinator's role on the part of middle managers.

Such shortcomings would need to be addressed if co-ordinators are to fulfil their potential to facilitate both individual and school development. The Mori survey on *The Continuing Professional Development of Teachers* (TTA 1995) confirmed that up to 1994–95 staff development was not being given the status it requires, but since then governmental initiatives to raise standards have promoted the importance of training and development (see OfSTED 1996; DfEE 1997a).

Perhaps there is a need for change in the perception of the co-ordinator's role by senior and middle managers if staff development is to become central to all that happens in schools. Were such a change to occur, co-ordinators would become integral to the school planning and appraisal process.

The problem of lack of time allocated to co-ordinators must be given serious consideration. Specific time could be planned for the extent of liaison required of co-ordinators, rather than the moments grabbed at lunch-time or after school. The problem can also be lessened by giving the role to a person without other major commitments. Help with administration would free-up time for more of the important aspects of the role. Also, a role specification would clarify the particular duties involved in the post. Training and support could be made available if schools and central government are actually as committed as they profess to professional development, and spending money to make it happen. A whole-school commitment to continuous development would ensure that all members of staff are aware of its importance. These problems are not insurmountable, given more widespread appreciation of the benefits staff development brings to all concerned. If they are not tackled, staff development will continue to remain a side issue and fail to reach its potential to bring about change (Rawlings 1997).

Process

Staff development priorities

A key issue for the staff development co-ordinator is establishing priorities (Wallace 1989). As a manager, the co-ordinator will need to engage in a decision-making process about matters identified in the following checklist.

1   Who should be involved in making decisions regarding professional development?
2   Who should be consulted about these decisions?
3   How may an appropriate balance be struck between needs at individual, group and whole-school levels?
4   What levels of priority are to be given to needs arising from national, LEA and school policies and to individual–personal interests and career aspirations, and the concern to improve the performance of present tasks?
5   What resources will be required to meet needs, such as supply-staff cover, staff training days, school budgets?
6   Will the staff feel able to cope with the additional pressures arising from the proposals?
7   What will be the impact on the pupils of their teachers being absent on INSET activities?
8   How are priorities to be communicated to staff and – as appropriate – to relevant people in the school cluster or pyramid, the LEA's INSET co-ordinator and advisers, and advisory teachers?

Management

A professional development co-ordinator will need to make time for informal discussions in which staff may state their needs. Indeed, it is important that such exchange of information takes place more formally through development interviews or the use of assessment forms. Release time and money for cover must be available to enable the co-ordinator to liaise adequately with staff. The differing needs of staff must be established so that informed decisions about staff and school development can be made. Formal interviews and appraisal can help this process. All of this is dependent on a commitment to staff development on the part of the senior management team. The contents of such formal and informal discussions will have to be monitored and evaluated regularly if they are to influence future development. The co-ordinator needs time to collate this information and to consider the opportunities for individual development within the overall plans of the school. Time is needed also to evaluate the effectiveness of developmental activities that do take place. Professional development planning should reflect the needs of the institution and of the individuals within it. This is possible only if the co-ordinator has sufficient information about all aspects of school development and adequate knowledge of the needs of each individual within the school (Rawlings 1997). An informed co-ordinator can use developmental opportunities for the benefit of both individuals and the school, and is of particular use here because of the understanding that comes with the role of just what, given the limitations of the school, is possible (ibid.).

Implementation

A range of activities can help the development of individuals and, if implemented across the organisation, the development of the school. The role of the co-ordinator is to suggest and help facilitate such development. This may require paying for cover, but the expense involved can be controlled by careful planning, bearing in mind also that teachers who are committed to some course of action can often organise themselves to enable it to happen. They do, however, need encouragement and permission to do so.

Many such possibilities for development depend on the general culture of the institution and the nature of its management. The development of individuals need not depend on expensive external courses, though it certainly does depend on less costly alternatives being recognised and utilised. It is in this capacity that the staff development co-ordinator, working with senior management, can make a difference to the lives and careers of individuals while also helping the school as a whole to develop (Rawlings 1997).

Choice of Course

Professional development has to be co-ordinated sensitively and realistically, but creatively, too, in the context of school development. Not everyone can do every course they want because of limited resources. The co-ordinator can, however, help staff to realise their potential by other means. Internal provision, according to Craft (1996), can be more successful than external courses because it meets the needs of particular individuals in a particular context. Monitoring the individuals who have and have not participated in developmental activities is also required. The co-ordinator must have an appreciation of all forms of school-based development and be familiar with the range of available external courses in order to encourage staff appropriately. Bids for developmental initiatives must be made, forms sent off to apply for appropriate courses and the necessary supply cover arranged (Rawlings 1997).

Action Plans

Once the staff development programme is implemented, the next key step is to ensure that there is appropriate follow-up action. Oldroyd and Hall (1991) claim that action plans can be of use here. An action plan is the link between training and follow-up. The action plan is the implementation process that will link new learning to practice in the school and classroom. Because such plans involve all levels of management, they may be implemented once agreed, thus saving the time and preventing the frustration that ensues when management veto brings to an end a carefully researched and presented proposal.

A good action plan needs to give detailed consideration not only to the innovation intended but to the strategy which will be employed to implement it. The process of planning is often more important than the plan. In terms of the innovation itself, the action plan might address the following questions:

1   Who will benefit from the change: pupils, myself, colleagues, others?
2   What will the costs be for those affected?
3   Is the envisaged change easy to communicate to those concerned and will they see its purpose?
4   Will it be possible to adapt the intended outcome to suit altered circumstances?
5   Will additional or new resources be required?

In terms of the strategy to implement the change, the following questions might help to focus the action plan:

1   Who needs to be aware of the intended outcome?
2   Whose support will be needed?
3   Are other key people to be given a sense of ownership of the change and their support thereby enlisted?
4   Are there other people with whom negotiation should be undertaken before the change is introduced?
5   By what means is feedback on progress best obtained?

An action plan (see Figure 1.2) should detail what is required, of whom and by when, in order for the outcome desired to be realised.

If the senior management team is committed to supporting the initiation of a developmental process, co-ordinators may have successfully negotiated a brief for the participants prior the start of the training. Whether or not this is the case, a debriefing session with the participants is important in order to focus on outcomes, intentions and possibilities. Key questions for a debriefing might be:

• What have you learned?
• What action do you intend to take as a result?
• What help might you need?
• Will you be able to disseminate some of the outcomes to non-participating colleagues?

Action Plan	
Target:	Staff:
Meetings: (dates)	Staff:
Completion Date:	
Monitoring Procedures	
Evaluation Procedures	
Review:	Staff:
Completion of Review (date):	Staff:
Disseminate to:	

Figure 1.2   Action plan

ADULT LEARNING

In order for professional development to be effective the co-ordinators should be aware of the needs of teachers as adult learners.

Many members of a school community will be committed to lifelong learning. Most will be graduates and a substantial number will be considering further study. The professional development co-ordinator and members of the senior management team will need to respect this expertise. Senior managers, too, should be aware of the differing styles of learning that teachers may pursue. Mumford (1997) points to four recognised learning styles and their respective types: activist; reflector; theorist; and pragmatist.

1   *Activists* learn best when exposed to new experiences. They like to get involved, tending to act first and consider the consequences later. They enjoy new challenges but are soon bored with the practicalities of implementation and the consolidations required. Activists will experiment with new techniques, use all the senses, enjoy talking things over, but dislike the rigour of research. They tend towards intuitiveness, seeing the whole picture and preferring to work out the consequences of alternative approaches to taking decisions on action plans. They are well suited to interactive courses and experiential learning, with high-profile activities and new challenges (e.g. use of role-play exercises), and limited listening to lectures and theoretical discourse or an involvement in too much detail.

2   *Reflectors* learn best from activities that allow them the time and space to ponder experiences and assimilate information before making a considered judgement. They tend towards cautiousness and spend time listening and observing. Opportunities for observation, listening, reviewing or researching without strict constraints on time or pressure to perform should be features of courses in which reflectors participate: flexitime study, for example.

3   *Theorists* learn best from activities that allow them to test theory on observations. They like to assimilate and classify information. They are analytical and are comfortable using theories and models to explain and understand data. They like detail, planning and rationality, but dislike intuitiveness and risk and are wary of working with others. Theorists will naturally be drawn to courses with a heavy theoretical component and time to investigate and question (e.g. arrange a seminar with other theorists); they tend to avoid learning activities that are unstructured and which lack conceptual depth and validation.

4   *Pragmatists* learn best from activities that have clear practical value and may be tested-out in action. They tend to dislike open-ended discussions. They make plans, want results, work well independently and like to solve problems in their own way without giving much attention to others' ideas. Pragmatists are well suited to practical and experiential learning in which they are led by someone with field experience in the subjects which really matter: for example, a course involving simulation and coaching through which they learn how to solve a real-life problem.

Honey and Mumford (1982) designed a questionnaire (see Appendix) the aim of which is to establish colleagues' preferred learning styles. Once it has been completed by all staff, co-ordinators and senior managers should analyse the data and consider the outcomes when planning the staff development programme.

Some people combine elements of these four types. Teams will, depending on size, feature more than one type, if not all four. Each type has a tendency to undervalue the skills of the other types, and this should be recognised by

22

both managers and team members. Co-ordinators and senior managers would need to consider:

- the situations which might be difficult for each type of learner;
- the extent of the influence of context on each type;
- the possibility of developing a more balanced learning style containing elements that will appeal to each type.

SUMMARY

This chapter has shown that the management of professional development in schools has much in common with the development of a learning organisation, created by a community in which everyone values learning and where quality is central to professional management and practice.

A learning organisation is one that is able to plan, set and meet targets. It is also a reflective organisation that is able to identify strengths, weaknesses, opportunities and threats and is professional in the way it manages and develops staff. Crucially, a learning organisation is one that is continually seeking ways in which to improve. It is in a learning organisation that professional development will be successful and effective.

Managers of professional development will recognise that teachers have careers that are more effective when managed. The need for continuous support in the development of a teacher's career is rooted in the changing role of education practitioners.

The management of professional development in schools will inevitably be dependent on the relationship between external and internal factors. The government and LEAs will have agendas that need to be met within the context of the school staff development policy. The importance of a supportive culture is also of considerable significance.

The challenge for the professional development co-ordinator, senior managers and staff is to know and understand the different needs of individuals and to have the skill and ability to meet each need in a collaborative and positive manner. Senior managers require an awareness of the differing styles of learning that exist.

In practice, professional development has to be clear and useful, with a focus on the question: what does development bring, in the best instances, to a professional career and to the institution? The link between developmental activity and follow-up is the key component that relates new learning to practice. A learning organisation will be effective in managing the professional development of its community.

Chapter 2 focuses on the relationship of TQM to the effective management of professional development in schools.

2

TQM AND THE MANAGEMENT
OF PROFESSIONAL
DEVELOPMENT

INTRODUCTION

The context in which practitioners work is also the setting in which professional development takes place. Teachers work for organisations that are corporate in their approach to management in terms of structure, communication and outcomes (Bolam 1999). Schools have teams to manage subjects, year groups, finance and other aspects of teaching and learning, and each team has a manager. The manager is recognised as having responsibility for co-ordinating his or her designated activity within the parameters set by the school. Schools are heavily dependent on the commitment of their employees in achieving targets, and much of what they do towards the achievement of high quality is completed in out of contract hours.

In practice, the school is a structured organisation that, with its ever-decreasing finances, places ever-increasing demands on its staff. Such a paradox creates a tension between internal and external goals and also between meeting the needs both of individuals and of the school. Tensions such as these are often compounded by complex changes, and practitioners and managers need to be prepared for such situations. The professional development of staff is a core activity that will contribute to a total quality organisation, a learning organisation.

This chapter focuses on total quality management (TQM) as advocated by Deming (1982) and Juran (1989). Beginning by defining TQM within human resource management (HRM), the chapter offers a detailed analysis of Handy's early definition of organisational culture. The importance of TQM and the development of teachers and schools are further developed in Chapter 3 in an examination of TQM in practice in a case-study school through the introduction of the Investors in People standard.

TOTAL QUALITY MANAGEMENT

Human resource management

In order to set the context for current TQM thinking, there is a need to consider definitions of HRM and accounts of its influence on education management. Not surprisingly, different meanings are associated with HRM. Storey (1992: 3) refers to HRM as 'a controversial ... phenomenon' because it is a focal point for diverse 'ideological, empirical [and] theoretical' concerns 'and, not least, the micro-politics of professional vested interest'.

The management of people as resources, on the one hand, and the management of resourceful human beings, on the other, describe the 'hard' and 'soft' ends of the continuum of HRM. At the 'hard' end of the continuum the emphasis is on people as resources to be rationalised. In contrast the 'soft' end of the continuum focuses on people as individuals to be supported and nurtured.

In practice, 'hard' HRM relates employees directly to the aims and objectives of the corporate or organisational strategy, where strategy is defined in terms of targets to be reached by all employees through management structures and reward systems. In contrast, the 'soft' approach is dependent on employee commitment and loyalty rather than on management and reward. In this soft HRM context employees are motivated by the task, the environment and the outcome, rather than by the management skills of their 'bosses' or financial rewards.

Defining Total Quality Management

TQM is an organisational or inter-organisational philosophy of continuous improvement achievable by people. It includes methods for leading and organising for quality, strategic planning, customer care, human resource development and structural problem solving. This concept was originally developed by two American statisticians, Deming and Juran, working in the Japanese manufacturing industry (Marsh 1991), and was rediscovered in America during the 1970s, moving to Britain in the 1980s. A plethora of management tools and techniques is associated with TQM, but the essence of total quality is that all employees are trained to regard themselves as suppliers of services to customers whose requirements must be defined, agreed and satisfied. There is a complete customer–supplier relationship between government, education and business: government funds the education sector which supplies organisations with an educated workforce, as well as providing industry with state-of-the-art research and development.

TQM consists of many elements, including leadership, information analysis, benchmarking, strategic quality planning, human resource development, quality results, quality assurance of products and services and

25

customer satisfaction. Before examining its primary aspects it is important to consider the '3 Cs' of TQM: culture; commitment; communication.

1   *Culture* is the sum of the rules, assumptions and values that bring an organisation together (Ott 1989; Mills and Murgatroyd 1991). In a successful TQM organisation, a culture exists in which

- innovation is valued highly;
- status is secondary to performance and contribution;
- leadership is a function of action, not position;
- rewards are shared through the work of teams;
- development, learning and training are seen as critical paths to sustainability;
- empowerment to achieve goals, supported by continued development and success, provide a climate for self-motivation.

Such a culture empowers the employees nearest the customer (in schools, teachers rather than senior management), and, it is argued, provides an enhanced sense of achievement and ownership. Culture is examined later in this chapter.

2   *Commitment* in a successful TQM organisation engenders a sense of pride and opportunity for development among its people (staff and customers) such that there is a great deal of ownership of organisational goals among and between all employees. Commitment is the norm rather than something exceptional or the result of some event of special personal significance. All employees are expected to display commitment to the organisation's goals. In schools, this requires of teachers a commitment to the success of the institution as well as to that of their subject or specific area of responsibility.

3   *Communication* in a successful TQM organisation is powerful, simple and effective both within and between teams. Such communication will be based on facts and genuine understanding rather than rumour and assumption. Effective communication is recognised as a vital management tool. It is no surprise, then, to find it an essential ingredient of Murgatroyd and Morgan's 1993 model for successful TQM in which the importance of open and free-flowing communication channels is emphasised.

TQM accords a fundamental significance to values and purpose: it is value-driven (Ormston 1996). TQM is concerned with managing the interpersonal components of organisations and acknowledges equally the interdependence between an organisation and its environment. In a TQM organisation people are trusted to work as professionals, and there is a strong emphasis on teamwork and a commensurably weak emphasis on hierarchy. Crucially, the organisation sets clear goals which are communicated effectively. As a consequence all members of the organisation have high expectations of themselves, and the organisation is 'fit for purpose'.

The customer or client is central to TQM organisations, and is defined as the person or group in receipt of a product or service. The organisation exists only for the customer; it has no other purpose. Once the customer's needs are known, systems are established to manage all processes. The emphasis is on prevention of mistakes and the elimination of poor quality. The appropriate procedures are defined by those who have the responsibility to implement them within clear organisational guidelines.

There is no one model for the structure of TQM organisations. What is important is that the structure should facilitate the task and process. The theoretical structure of a TQM organisation involves a coalition of autonomous teams able to interact directly with the customer and with each other. These are all linked to senior management teams responsible for strategy.

TQM leaders have a vision which is articulated to the organisation. Leaders are creative and sensitive, empowering people through delegation and training. TQM leaders emphasise change, leading their organisation so that it becomes a change agent rather than a changed organisation. The organisation becomes a learning organisation, integrating personal and organisational development. The emphasis of TQM is therefore on the development of people, leaders as well as followers, in order to achieve individual and organisational goals.

Teams are fundamental to TQM. Members of TQM teams have explicit and shared values. Leadership of the team is based on function and need rather than power and status. There is pride in belonging to a team the aims and task of which are clear. Crucially the team learns and develops by a process of continuous feedback and review. This process is characterised by a high degree of openness and candour. Essential decisions are shared. Teams have full commitment and are action focused. When TQM is applied to organisations, is is teams that make things happen!

Reflection on these general observations should serve to make clear the value of TQM to educational institutions. Education in schools is driven by a political ideology rooted in success. All pupils must learn; the knowledge and skills they gain through schooling are measured; and these, in turn, are indicators of how teachers perform (DfEE 1999).

Quality is manifested through the achievement of targets set by inspectors (HMI–OfSTED), local education authorities (LEA) and school management teams. There is a fundamental need for practitioners to share in the measuring of the quality their teaching provides. Targets need to be shared by all in order that quality in practice is achieved. Dale and Cooper (1992: 2) state:

> For the word ['quality'] to have the desired effect as intended by
> the user, and to prevent any form of misunderstanding in commu-
> nication ... the person using the word must have a clear
> understanding of its meaning, those to whom the communication is

directed should have a similar understanding. When quality is discussed within an organisation, to prevent confusion and ensure that everyone in each department is focused on the same objectives, there should be an organisational definition of quality.

Quality therefore

- is not negotiable;
- is all-pervasive;
- increases productivity;
- leads to better performance in the marketplace.

From the above, it can be deduced that TQM cannot be superimposed *on* an existing management system or *within* an existing culture. TQM is a holistic management approach which applies to all levels of an organisation, to every relationship and every process.

FEATURES OF TOTAL QUALITY MANAGEMENT ORGANISATIONS

Myer and Zucker (1989) identify five features critical to successful TQM organisations; these enable what Murgatroyd (1991) later defined as sustainable steep-slope quality improvement. These are:

1   Alignment within the organisation [everyone working towards achieving an organisation's goals] or commitment to a shared vision. This can be achieved through the creation of mission statements which staff use to underpin all their actions. A successful TQM organisation will have a mission statement that is owned and enacted by all of the stakeholders in the equation.
2   An extended understanding of the customer-driven and process-orientated basis for quality. The experience of TQM organisations suggests that improvement to the detail of customer-driven processes leads to enhanced service provision. Consequently the focus on the process owner/provider is an essential element in TQM.
3   Team focus. A TQM organisation is designed around teams, invests in teams and measures outcomes against the performance of teams. The TQM approach underlines the central importance of devolving process management, and indeed target determination, to trusted and empowered teams.
4   Target setting. The setting of targets, including challenging or unlikely goals, will commit an organisation to the significant improvement that results from their pursuit. Target setting is a common feature in advo-

28

cated management styles, and indeed is emerging as a prerequisite for schools in the late 1990s. While achievable targets are a necessity in the management of any organisation and its employees, targets from the 'challenge zone' engender feelings of worth, trust in potential, and if achieved, a sense of accomplishment.

5   Systematic management through effective communication and performance measurement. The management, measurement and manifestation, through information provision, of achievements and developments are essential to successful TQM. Furthermore, there is a requirement to regularly review and reflect upon progress in order to maintain improvement.

These features reflect the common principles outlined by Dale and Cooper (1992). Murgatroyd and Morgan (1993) inverted these criteria for success to form negative statements outlining factors common to failing organisations:

(1)   There is no shared vision or commitment to the organisation's goal; people operate in disconnected, sometimes contradictory, ways.
(2)   Quality is the rhetoric rather than the product of the organisation, and the organisation's strategy concentrates on self-perpetuation rather than self-improvement.
(3)   Teamwork does not exist; instead a rigid hierarchy encourages internecine conflict and competition.
(4)   Goals are set, but tend to be short-term and within the 'comfort zone' rather than the 'challenge zone'; such goals are based on outcomes rather than processes.
(5)   Mediocrity and conformance have become acceptable to the organisation.
(6)   Feedback to employees about the effectiveness of their contribution is minimal. Communication tends to be one-way – top-down.

Successful TQM relies upon the key features of vision, strategy and teamwork in order to achieve a range of challenging goals/targets and regular systematic management.

Management

A fundamental requirement for the success of TQM is commitment at the highest levels of an organisation's management to the principles and practices of TQM (Marsh 1991; Dale and Cooper 1992). Without this commitment, TQM processes are likely to lack permanence or validity within the organisation's culture. The creation and maintenance of a culture conducive to continuous quality improvement into which each individual subscribes is also a vital element in the TQM equation. Murgatroyd and Morgan (1993: 5) state:

> The key word in TQM is management. Quality performance does not occur by happen chance or accident, it occurs because it is designed into the way an organisation works; it permeates all aspects of the organisation.

It is not the technique that is so crucial but the process of question-and-answer through which the technique leads the executive team. This leads to a much greater depth of strategic understanding and an actual commitment to total quality. However, a factor that contributes to the success of TQM is the measurement of progress against both internal and external benchmarks or indicators. The recognition of progress by all participants is perhaps best facilitated through setting clear short-term targets from which a development planning cycle springs; thus change and development are incremental. Juran (1989) is in favour of tackling 'elephant-sized' projects by dividing them into 'bite-sized' assignments, thereby creating a series of achievable short-term targets.

Total quality means what it says: all aspects of the organisation are dedicated to the achieving of the standards of performance required by their customers (internal or external). TQM requires a systematic management of supplier–customer relationships. What is important here is that attention is given to the managing of *processes*, because processes produce outcomes. Here 'process' refers to the way in which people work to achieve results. Outcomes follow processes. Enhanced outcomes follow from the quality of management applied to the detail of the processes of the organisation's many internal supplier–customer relationships.

This also encompasses the sustainable steep slope of quality improvement. Not all organisations can achieve sustainability. Steep-slope TQM aims at significant and substantive quality and performance improvements, not just small marginal gains. Steep-slope quality improvement across a number of performance indicators (in schools, for example, student and parent satisfaction, social behaviour, attendance, self-esteem, leaving performance) can be achieved only by a consistent and focused commitment to quality performance. Hart (1998: 22) states that what is at issue here is

> high performing schools achieving the level of their added value not their absolute gains ... so that it is the amount of 'added value' to the initial position that counts as performance. TQM holds out as much promise for performance gains in schooling as it has achieved in other endeavours.

Without its integration with strategy, TQM becomes in effect a 'bolt-on'. A process is required which translates the strategy through to a TQM action plan. An element crucial to successful TQM is the process that links corporate organisational strategy to the TQM plan. The management team must select a method suitable to that plan and apply it continuously.

Management commitment must be reflected in action and not just rhetoric. This means pro-active participation in all of the elements of TQM. Management commitment to TQM can also be measured in the size of its budget. TQM focuses on excellence through quality management.

It is essential that TQM is adapted to fit the organisation and not the other way round. In order for TQM to succeed:

1   Quality of leadership and strength of management are essential.
2   People need to *belong*, to be *valued* and to *participate*.
3   *All work is a process*, involving customers, suppliers, resources and controls.
4   The basic principles of problem solving need to be acknowledged.

Teams

There is now an 'empowerment through teams' movement that has a strong hold on education management thinking. Teams are considered desirable for their potential to maximise the creative talent within a learning organisation. By planning learning at the centre teams become learning units that encourage the transfer of knowledge and skills. In practice, teams promote ownership. Through ownership teams are able to problem-solve cross-functionally by assigning a problem to an individual team member. Teamwork also carries lobbying powers in terms of teams collaborating in support of proposals that will lead to change. Such features are conditional on four things:

(a)   a commitment to teamworking from the top of the organisation;
(b)   investment in training and development to help teams to master the skills of effective team working;
(c)   that teams are the basic unit for dealing with all activities within the organisation;
(d)   teams being given very specific mandates, deadlines and resources to perform their tasks responsibly and effectively.

The team is empowered to determine how it will achieve the goal it has been given in the context of a shared vision and understanding – in a climate of trust.

The TQM perspective requires organisations to regard themselves as good at what they do and able to exceed their own expectations about their performance. For success, teams have to undertake a great deal of new learning. In schools, the goals focus primarily on process outcomes, completion of learning targets in less time, increasing the percentage of pupils meeting performance targets, new learning activities, new modes of teaching, etc., rather than on profitability. Each goal should apply to all in the organisation, not just some, and be directly measurable. If TQM is to succeed there is a need for investment in learning for all.

IMPLICATIONS FOR SCHOOLS

The general implication for schools is that, to adopt TQM principles, they must introduce new structures and approaches to management, teaching and learning (Glasser 1990; Holt 1993; Schomoker and Wilson 1993).

Perhaps the most influential work analysing TQM is *Out of the Crisis* (Deming 1982). In it he outlined fourteen points he regarded as vital if an organisation was to prosper. Deming's fourteen points for TQM are:

1   Create constancy of purpose for improvement of the product and the service, with the aims to become competitive, stay in business and provide jobs. This requires long-term planning and the flexibility to meet the constantly changing needs of the customers.
2   Adopt the new philosophy. This means adopting new ways of working which promote quality.
3   Cease dependence on mass inspection to achieve quality. Inspection does not guarantee quality. Instead employees should be empowered with the training, skills and methods to assess and improve their own quality of output.
4   With regard to suppliers, end the practice of awarding business on the basis of price. Competitive tendering, which is largely price-based, inter-feres with the development of long-standing qualitative relationships with suppliers, and working closely with them on the quality of their provision.
5   Improve constantly and forever the system of production and service in order to improve quality and productivity, and thus to constantly decrease costs.
6   Institute on-the-job training. Unless training is relevant to the organisa-tion, it can prove wasteful. The training and development of the workforce against a fixed standard of what is deemed acceptable work is an essential part of an organisation's success.
7   Institute leadership: 'the job of management is not supervision, but leadership' (Deming 1982: 1). This means a shift away from manage-ment concern with outcomes to a role which encourages improvement in the processes involved in creating quality goods and services.
8   Drive out fear, so that everyone can work effectively for the company. It is important for the purpose of motivating staff that they should feel secure in their working environment.

9   Break down barriers between departments. This assists in achieving unity of purpose.
10 Eliminate slogans, exhortations and targets asking for new levels of productivity without providing the workforce with the methods to do the job better.
11 Eliminate work standards that prescribe numerical quotas. These promote a focus on output of processes, rather than inputting quality into working practices.
12 Remove barriers that rob people of their right to pride of workmanship. (Deming argues that appraisal systems should be abolished because they put staff in competition with each other and impact negatively on team-work.)
13 Institute a vigorous programme of education and self-improvement. Better-educated staff are better able to undertake quality improvements.
14 Put everyone in the company to work to accomplish the transformation. All individuals have responsibility for transforming the workplace culture to one of quality, and overseeing this transformation is the most important role for management.

Each of the above serves to illustrate that total quality management is concerned with processes which enact a philosophy of continuous improvement in which all the participants share the commitment to deliver a 'high quality' product or service to their customers or stakeholders.

TQM approaches are increasingly promoted in educational literature as tools for school improvement (Paine, Turner and Pryke 1992; Barker 1993; Bostingl 1993; Murgatroyd and Morgan 1993). It is clear that TQM principles are increasingly informing the management of schools, and the benefits are felt by pupils and staff. The focus on continuous improvement – 'yearning for learning' (Bostingl 1993) – is regarded as a crucial feature in the applicability of TQM principles to schools. Sevick (1993) argues that TQM is relevant to education because it asserts the centrality of pupil welfare and development, creates a better learning environment by reducing competitiveness (both internal and external), and because building educational quality *during* the process is less costly than attempting to build it through inspection at the *end* of the process. Any practical application of TQM principles requires schools to engage in short- and long-term planning, staff training and development and continuous assessment, while introducing quality improvement teams and ensuring management commitment (Terry 1996). Proponents of TQM argue that it contributes to the continuous improvement of schools because they become characterised by unity, change and trust. Schools using TQM report such 'hard' benefits as reduced drop-out rates and better test scores (Terry 1996). The growing success of the total quality movement in education is due, in some part, to the high level of involvement it requires of the key players in each educational institution: the quality movement concentrates its efforts and energies on school governance, curriculum design, instructional practices and student outcomes (Leuenberger, Whitaker and Sheldon 1993).

It should, however, be acknowledged that introducing TQM into schools is undoubtedly a challenge. Blankstein and Swain (1994) examined the introduction of Deming's TQM principles to a Florida elementary school, and reported that the key obstacles to be surmounted were:

- overcoming resistance to change
- leadership misconceptions
- reliance on external motivators (promotions and grades)
- increased training costs
- emotion-driven decision making
- restrictions imposed by state (government) mandates
- somewhat mechanical application of TQM principles.

Indeed, the mechanical application of TQM principles reduces what should be an innovative and forward-looking process to the kind of administrative treadmill which issues in team and measurement mania.

Capper and Jamison (1993) warn that the worthy principles underpinning TQM can be a force for negative management, as expressed through coercion and control. Quong and Walker (1996) have indicated the shortcomings of importing a philosophy without having a real commitment to its principles; they agree with Hixson and Lovelace's assertion (1993) that TQM does offer a philosophical and practical basis for restructuring – provided it is thoughtfully applied.

A MODEL FOR PRACTICE

Murgatroyd and Morgan (1993) present a model for the practical implementation of TQM principles in schools which is based on three ingredients: trust; leadership commitment; empowerment.

Trust has to be earned. Trust is the basis on which depend many aspects of the 3 Cs of the organisation's culture.

Leadership commitment must be visible. All leaders are required to demonstrate their commitment to TQM and its implications in all of their actions all of the time. Rather than interpreting their function to be that of controlling and ensuring the implementation of a given policy, leaders need to secure a sense of visionary possibility in the organisation. Traditional forms of leadership in schools have often been characterised by

- fast-track solutions to problems
- the assumption that change happens in modest and moderate increments

- a tendency to plan after the event for the next occurrence
- maximising being rational
- a submissive posture by majority
- an acceptance of the system – we are the victims of history and of decisions taken elsewhere; there is little we can do to shape our own strategy.

As Sergiovanni (1990) has pointed out, TQM leadership requires a very different set of assumptions about management and the work of managers:

- TQM leadership is about imagination – the enabling and empowerment of the rank and file – not about status.
- The role of the TQM leader is to activate staff so that they focus on a shared vision, their strategy and set of intended outcomes.
- TQM visionary leaders realise that it is cost effective to empower those nearest to a process to manage that process themselves.
- TQM leaders concentrate on the whole picture and keep it at the forefront of people's thinking.
- TQM leaders are prepared to search for the small things that can make a critical difference.
- TQM leaders believe that challenge and fun go together – laughter is healing.

Empowerment. Most schools are hierarchically managed. Schein (1984) considered that in Britain, there is a tradition of organisations in which

- truth comes from those with positional power;
- people need to be directed in the carrying out of instructions and supervised to enact commitments;
- relationships in the main are linear and vertical;
- each person has a niche that cannot be invaded;
- the organisation is responsible for taking care of its members.

The model outlined in Figure 2.1 indicates the interaction between teams, tools and the strategy or goals of the organisation, and the dependence upon a culture which creates the circumstances (through commitment and communication) which impact on the vision of the organisation. Murgatroyd and Morgan (1993), as we have seen, argue for the centrality of trust, leadership and empowerment. Arguably, true empowerment implies leadership that entrusts an organisation's development or improvement to all of its stakeholders. Leadership of this nature needs a visionary ingredient which constantly posits the art of the possible in the organisation's consciousness, but also requires that leaders take a wide-ranging role in enabling employees to fulfil their own and the collective potential. An adaptation of Murgatroyd and Morgan's list of leadership

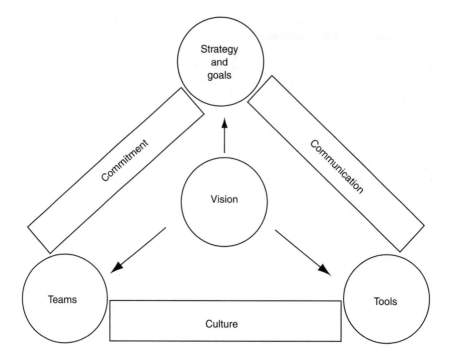

Figure 2.1   Model for TQM in schools

Source Murgatroyd and Morgan (1993), © Open University Press

qualities would define TQM leadership as imaginative and sensitive; one that activates, coaches, guides, mentors, educates, assists, supports, enables and empowers colleagues to focus upon a shared vision and to manage their processes to achieve the organisation's challenging collective goals. This constitutes a demanding list, but one that illustrates the fundamental philosophy that underpins TQM.

Trust, leadership and empowerment relate directly to culture. A learning organisation will sustain and build on a learning community. Yet a learning community will not function to its potential in a culture that is not conducive to TQM.

CULTURE

Given that TQM pertains to all areas of an organisation, the contribution of a culture that infiltrates even the most sceptical reaches of that organisation should not be underestimated. This requires considerable care and thought, and is perhaps the most significant challenge in introducing TQM, as changing and managing people's attitudes and behaviour require considerable skill. The outcome of this cultural shift should be that employees work against inertia by assuming that processes can be improved, learn from mistakes and, perhaps most crucially, recognise their relationships with internal customers, whereby tasks performed for individuals within an organisation are deemed of equal importance to those for external customers. Education and training offer an avenue to increase awareness of TQM concepts and to develop the skills which will empower employees to implement TQM practices, thereby contributing to a shift in attitudes. Schein (1992) constructed a formal definition of organisational culture derived from a dynamic model of learning that relates clearly to educational practice:

1   Culture is always in the process of formation and change;
2   Culture tends to cover all aspects of human functioning;
3   Culture is learned around the major issues of external adaptation and internal integration;
4   Culture is ultimately embraced as an interrelated, patterned set of basic assumptions that deal with ultimate issues, such as the nature of humanity and human relationships.... The nature of the workplace requires consideration in the context of the nature of reality and truth itself.

When schools are developing as learning organisations, practitioners will need to recognise that organisation and culture do not have the same meaning. Ogbonna (1992: 72), citing Burrell and Morgan (1979), found that 'culture is something an organisation *is* and, culture is something an organisation *has*'.

This statement implies that, as an organisation changes, so will the culture in terms of what it *is*; however, as the organisation changes, the culture it *has* may remain the same. Such quandaries may be manifest in the organisation's resistance to change, in practice or from its leadership. For example, if a school's management team has a change of membership, staff perceptions and behaviours may remain unchanged: the organisation has changed but the culture has not.

At the point when change is being considered, organisational managers would need to reflect on the three levels of cultural phenomena as defined by Schein (1984, in Ogbanna 1992: 76):

1   On the surface are the overt behaviours and other physical manifestations (artefacts and creations).
2   Below this level is a sense of what 'ought' to be (values).
3   At the very deepest level are those things that are taken for granted as 'correct' ways of coping with the environment (basic assumptions).

Foy (1981) suggested that managers should try to understand the culture of their organisation because they will be better able to relate to the organisation if they appreciate its nature, and may be able to predict the behaviour of people in the organisation.

THE CULTURE OF SCHOOLS

The culture of a school is its 'personality', manifested in the way that work is done. Every school is different and has slightly different expectations of its management. A school culture will manifest itself in many forms:

practices	rites, rituals and ceremonies
communications	stories, myths, sagas, legends, folk tales, symbols and slogans
physical forms	location, style and condition of the school buildings, fixtures and fittings
common language	the phrases or jargon common to the school.

Further, within each culture, subcultures exist, with their own sets of characteristics. The school culture may be the dominant culture, while subject or year teams may create their own subcultures.

Handy (1993) provides a detailed examination of cultural issues relating to schools as organisations which may provide readers with viewpoints from which to consider their own schools. Handy identified three aspects of organisations – power, people and politics – which he believed should

> *help to explain the past*, which in turn
> *helps to understand the present*, and thus
> *to predict the future*, which leads to
> *more influence over future events*, and
> *less disturbance from the unexpected.*

Organisations differ in their ways of working. Handy defined differences in their levels of authority, formality and control; their varying degrees of planning; their distinctive financial systems, rules and results. Handy also described the impact on organisations of the buildings they occupy (schools can certainly offer variety here). The most significant focus, however, is on the people within organisations, as it is they who create and work within the culture of an organisation. Handy perceived organisations as collections of individuals and political systems, joined together by power and influence.

Handy (1993) defined a framework for the analysis of organisational practice in terms of the four cultures identified with the lists set out below. The lists are compilations of common characteristics of organisational culture as Handy saw it, but which serve usefully to illuminate analysis of the culture of schools. Each list contains elements that apply to TQ organisations, but these are not exhaustive. When applied to schools the characteristics may be more observable at different periods of the school day, week or year! The following can be used as a checklist from which an analysis of a school's culture can begin:

The Power Culture

A power culture is one that is led by a 'Zeus-like' leader, controlling from the centre of the organisational web. The characteristics of a power culture are:

- entrepreneurial and small
- web shaped in design

- would have as its patron god Zeus – the god of the broad light of day
- culture depends on a central figure from whom rays of power and influence emanate
- organisational effectiveness depends on trust and empathy
- communication happens via personal conversation and telepathy
- if the central figure has chosen well, staff can be left to get on with the job
- few rules and procedures – little bureaucracy
- control is exercised by occasional forays from the centre or summonses to the centre
- proud and strong, the central figure can move quickly in response to threats or danger
- the quality of the person(s) at the centre is of paramount importance
- employees will prosper and be satisfied if they are power-orientated, politically minded and rate risk-taking as important
- financial and human resources are the major power base
- limited security
- restricted in size because the web is weakened progressively as it seeks to extend
- involved in limited range of activities
- places faith in the individual, not in committees
- judges by results and is tolerant of their means

- low morale and high turnover in the middle layers which tend to be overly competitive

As this list indicates, a power culture is one that is controlling rather then empowering, and is determined by the person at the centre of the web.

The Role Culture

A more democratic approach to organisations is the role culture. Within a role culture structures and systems allow teams greater breadth of activity supported by a firm base, as represented by the pillars in a Greek temple.

The characteristics of a role culture are:

- stereotypically bureaucratic
- logical and rational – its patron god would be Apollo, the god of reason
- strength is in its pillars, its middle managers
- the work of the pillars, and the interaction between them, is controlled by procedures which regulate roles (job descriptions, authority decisions), communications (requisite sets of memos) and the settling of disputes
- co-ordinated from the top by a narrow band of senior managers
- the role or job description is more important than the individual
- individuals are selected for satisfactory performance in the role, and performance over and above the role is not required
- positional power is the major power source
- personal power is frowned upon and expert power merely tolerated
- rules and procedures are the major methods of exerting influence
- needs a stable environment, e.g. civil service
- offers security and predictability – clear career path
- economies of scale are more important than flexibility
- slow to perceive the need for change
- change might lead to collapse and the need for new management

The structures and systems of a role culture are its strengths, though they can be its weaknesses in certain conditions. The effectiveness of a role culture is dependent on the ability to manage of each team leader.

The Task Culture

A task culture is driven by the expertise of individuals in relation to the task. Its characteristics include:

- orientation to the job or project and an emphasis on getting the job done
- its structure is best described as a net

- some strands of the net are thicker and stronger than others
- influence is based on expertise more than on personal power
- utilises the unifying power of the group to ensure that individuals identify with the objective of the organisation
- has groups, project teams or task forces for specific purposes
- work is highly controlled
- easy working relationships within groups, with mutual respect based upon capability rather than age or status, which are appropriate where flexibility and sensitivity are required
- limited range of expertise
- thrives in contexts where speed of reaction, integration, sensitivity and creativity are important
- not easy to control – what control is achieved is by allocation of projects
- little day-to-day management
- tends to be attractive to middle managers
- lack of resources can lead to political problems
- not always the culture most appropriate to the prevailing climate and the predominant technology

Given the multiplicity of tasks performed in schools, the adoption of a role culture would necessitate close and careful management. The relationship between the school and its external environment would also impact on this model.

The Person Culture

The freedom of a person culture allows for creativity and growth. For a co-operative organisation like a small school this may be appropriate. As an organisational culture for larger schools it would be difficult to manage. Its characteristics would include:

- the individual is the focus
- can attract unusual individuals, who might thereafter cling to its values
- it exists only to serve and assist the individuals within it
- structure best described as a cluster

- control mechanisms are ineffective
- influence is shared; the power-base is usually expert; individuals do what they are good at
- generally only the creative achieve success
- individual personnel may belong also to other cultures – not easy to manage and not easily impressed, little influence can be brought on them

It should be noted that in the context of TQM each of these lists would require further analysis relating to customer needs. The adoption of any one particular culture would also need to be determined by its suitability to the task.

SUMMARY

This chapter has introduced the principles of TQM and its relevance to schools as an organisational or inter-organisational philosophy of continuous improvement achieved by people. It includes methods for leading and organising for quality, strategic planning, customer care, human resource development and structural problem solving.

In essence, TQM is value-driven (Ormston 1996). It is concerned with managing the interpersonal components of organisations and acknowledges equally the interdependence of the organisation and its environment. Within a TQM organisation, people are trusted to work as professionals, and there is a strong emphasis on teamworking and a correspondingly weak emphasis on hierarchy. Crucially, the organisation sets clear goals which are communicated effectively. As a consequence members of the organisation have high expectations of themselves, and the organisation is 'fit for purpose'. Despite the encouragement of the quality movement, the introduction of TQM into schools is undoubtedly a challenge.

Given that TQM pertains to all areas of the organisation, the potential contribution of a culture that infiltrates even the most sceptical reaches of that organisation should not be underestimated. The definition of cultural characteristics, compiled from Handy (1993), may be used as a checklist from which an analysis of a school's organisational culture can begin.

The general implication for schools wishing to adopt TQM principles is that they must introduce new structures and approaches to management, teaching and learning. The principles having been considered, the next chapter examines TQM in practice through a consideration of a secondary school's application to register for the Investor in People standard.

3

INVESTORS IN PEOPLE

INTRODUCTION

The previous chapter offered a definition of TQM, emphasising its importance in relation to the management of professional development in schools. This chapter builds on the importance of TQM principles to a learning organisation through an examination of the Investors in People (IIP) standard. A description of the IIP standard is followed by a case study of a school's application to retain the standard it had achieved in 1996.

Investors in People (IIP) is a Department for Education and Employment (DfEE) initiative administered by the Training and Enterprise Council through regional centres. The scheme was designed by the Confederation of British Industry (CBI) in consultation with leading professional and business organisations, trades unions and the Institute of Personnel Management (IPM). It was developed by the National Training Task Force (NTTF) and launched on a national scale in 1990. The CBI and NTTF considered that the British economy would better meet the changing demands of the global economy were organisations and institutions to put more emphasis on staff investment and development.

The National Education and Training Task Force target is for 70 per cent of all organisations with 200 or more employees and 35 per cent of those employing 50 or more to be recognised as Investors in People by 2000.

The IIP standard aims to help organisations and institutions of all kinds to improve their performance and effectiveness by realising the full potential of their workforce. The sector with the fastest growth in take-up of IIP is currently that of schools. It is recognised that the IIP standard contributes the best business practice combining to inform staff development.

The four principles on which IIP is based are:

1   commitment from the top levels of the organisation to develop all employees to meet its strategic objectives;
2   planning and reviewing the training and development needs of employees;

3 action to train and develop individuals on recruitment and throughout their employment; and
4 evaluation to access the achievement resulting from investment in training and development to improve future effectiveness.

The cycle of continuous improvement emphasises schools as learning organisations, providing unity of purpose and clarity of vision. As with TQM, the IIP principles involve all employees in reviewing practice and setting targets. The IIP standard seeks to improve performance through people, while setting the level of 'good practice' in the organisation.

TQM AND IIP

The relationship of TQM to IIP is described in the following analysis: the principles of IIP clearly exhibit a concern which is consistent with an organisation's goals, and the effective management and maintenance of that culture (Legge 1989). Such apparent contradictions in putting theory into practice are well documented (Legge 1989; Lloyd and Rawlinson 1992; Ogbonna 1992), and, inevitably, school organisations have to retain some flexibility to respond to changed circumstances.

Similarly, IIP requires schools to reflect on their quality assurance procedures. Diverse quality assurance methods are currently practised in schools, ranging from OfSTED inspections, appraisal procedures and assessment of teacher competences, to the public examinations' system.

The introduction of the National Curriculum (1988–92) was itself an example of an attempt to ensure the delivery of quality education across schools in the state sector. The increased autonomy granted to schools through Local Management of Schools (LMS) led them also to reflect on their performance. This has been furthered through the publication of formal examination results in league tables and the government's requirement that LEAs and schools set targets for improved performance in the core subjects of English, Mathematics and Science in 1999, and in all subjects by 2000.

A further link between TQM and IIP is their mutual interest in the relationship that obtains between the organisation and its customers. Schools have had to recognise their place in a chain of service provision in which both the consumers and the providers of that service have become more sophisticated and more demanding as a result of enhanced choice. This reflects the movement towards market-driven public services, where organisations are expected to meet quality assurance standards and add value through developmental planning. Quality is no longer the preserve of the expert or the professional body; rather it is increasingly defined by the expectations of customer and stakeholder alike (Oakland 1989; Atkinson 1991; Berry 1991).

Murgatroyd and Morgan (1993) identified three main contributors to the definition of quality in schools: quality assurance standards or indicators; contracted performance by participants and stakeholders; and customer expectations of quality. There is a suggestion that customer-defined quality is emerging as the principal factor in the equation, supported by 'contract conformance' (i.e. meeting the demands of negotiated contracts) 'and quality assurance' (ibid.).

The impact of TQM on practice is an inversion of the traditional hierarchical management pyramid illustrated in Figure 3.1, in which senior management is represented at the apex of the triangle and therefore as of most importance; teachers, who directly provide the service, are in the middle; and customers are at the bottom (Quong and Walker 1996; Sallis 1996). In the TQM model it is the teacher who, as closest to the point of delivery, is seen to be best able to deliver quality improvement to the customer stakeholders. The role of management in the inverted hierarchy will be focused on developing the internal supplier–customer working practices (Murgatroyd and Morgan 1993), and devising strategies to enable teachers to meet the expectations of the customer/consumer base and identify their needs.

The setting of short-term targets underpins both IIP and TQM approaches to staff and school development. Furthermore, the IIP indicators, through their emphasis on continuous development and improvement, force institutions away from customary or *ad hoc* ways of doing things. The IIP and TQM provision of series of externally validated benchmark indicators moves organisations towards a shared understanding of how best to manage and develop their workforce, and away from a reliance on hypothesised connections between human resource policy choices and the associated set of outcomes (Beer et al. 1985).

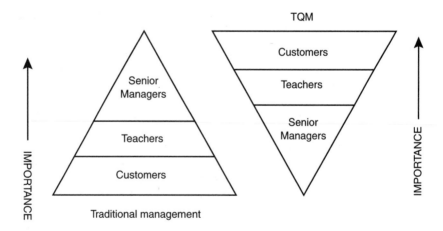

Figure 3.1 The inverted pyramid of TQM

Source: Hart (1998), adapted from Sallis (1996: 31)

THE IMPACT OF IIP IN SCHOOLS

The sector of fastest growth in the take-up of IIP currently is schools (Brown and Taylor 1996). Thames Valley TEC is among those successfully persuading schools to apply for the IIP standard. The TEC argues that the IIP standard constitutes the best business practice combining to inform staff development, and that the four principles upon which IIP is based transfer appropriately to schools. Brown and Taylor (1996: 371) state:

> The IIP standard assists schools in transforming themselves further, by looking for ways of improving their operating procedures and processes and getting the best out of staff by motivating them to feel committed and valued, by giving them an understanding of what their contribution can be to the school as a whole and the skills to fulfil their potential.

Schools which by 1994 had achieved, or had been working towards achieving, the IIP standard reported (TES 1994) on the benefits of the Investors' process. Among the positive outcomes were that the process

- gives schools an opportunity and focus for involving all staff in school development planning;
- indicates to all staff that they are valuable members of the institution;
- allows schools to identify gaps in internal communication patterns and to take steps to close them;
- focuses on the professional development model for staff appraisal and helps to demonstrate to staff that this model best meets individual and organisational training and development needs;
- brings school staff into contact with staff in other organisations/institutions working towards the same standard.

Zienau (1996) points to further benefits to schools, which include:

- Funding is available to subsidise work in school;
- The IIP standard demands that consultants help the school leaders to examine the realities of life within the organisation they lead;
- The discipline and structure required by the process are helpful in making clear to school staff the consultants' objectives and success criteria.
- External assessment based on systematic and consistent principles permits schools to partake successfully in the process.

The five features of TQM identified by Dale and Cooper (1992) provide a framework within which to examine the implications of IIP for TQM principles in the school context:

1   *Vision*: IIP requires the shared understanding of organisational goals and the alignment within the school of individual development so as to achieve those goals. This is more sophisticated than simply creating a mission statement: it requires that development is holistic, so that all staff are included in the developmental planning equation, from agreeing training targets to the provision of training and the evaluation of its outcomes within the context of the school's goals.

2   *Strategy*: IIP impacts on school strategy because it requires schools to build training and improvement into developmental planning. Moreover, it requires schools to provide evidence of their strategies for training and development, and the assessment involves establishing that these strategies are functioning meaningfully in the school.

3   *Teamwork*: the hierarchical structure of schools does not impinge as harshly as might be expected on the implications of IIP or TQM principles. Developing responsibility for training to line manager level contributes to the departmental team approach to identifying training and development needs. The key to ensuring successful TQM in this instance is to ensure that departmental team planning for training and development interconnects with the objectives of whole-school development. The creation of quality development teams, which now exist in most schools, has contributed to this synergy.

4   *Setting targets*: the importance of setting of targets is immediately apparent in the IIP literature. The first principle, *commitment*, requires the school to set its aims and objectives through planning and evaluation; and thereafter target setting is integral to all processes. IIP requires that the school has a written training and development plan which identifies the needs of the school's personnel and the actions to meet those needs. IIP requires also the setting of targets for training and development at all levels of the school. Significant, too, is the clear expectation that employees are involved in setting their own training targets.

5   *Systematic daily management*: the framework of IIP demands that the systems of training and development are established through four principles – commitment, planning, action and evaluation. In order to achieve the standard, systems have to be in place to ensure that the IIP process operates successfully. However, that process does not manage itself, and it is necessary to manage systems in order to maintain it. These systems must consist of *activities* which encompass each of the four principles.

IIP IN PRACTICE

The IIP standard, administered and assessed locally by TECs and in Scotland by Local Enterprise Companies (LECs), provides a manual to assist employers in gathering the evidence for the portfolio submitted as part of the assessment process. The stages of assessment are these:

1   *Formal commitment* by the organisation to the standard. For this stage, the tool kit provides institutions with a manager survey and an employee survey. The manager survey requires senior managers to score their organisations against the national standard. The employee survey takes the form of a questionnaire, the aim of which is to elicit employee opinions of staff development policies and practices, and of the commitment of senior management to invest in staff.

2   An *action plan* is drawn up to address the gap perceived between the requirements of the IIP standard and the practices currently operating within the organisation. A letter of commitment from the chief executive (in the case of schools, the headteacher) to the local TEC publicly obliges the institution to put the plan into action.

3   *Implementation* of the action plan to improve the policies, procedures and practices of the organisation against the IIP's benchmark indicators.

4   The organisation *gathers evidence* and compiles a portfolio to show that it is now meeting the standard. A licensed assessor visits the organisation to assess this evidence and to interview a cross-section of employees.

5   If the *evaluation* proves satisfactory, the assessor recommends the organisation to the local IIP assessment panel. If the performance of the organisation is regarded as meeting the requirements of the standard, the organisation is recognised. Otherwise the recognition is withheld pending further improvements to those areas in which the organisation failed to meet the standard's requirements. Deferred recognition usually indicates that the organisation has failed to meet the benchmarks set out in the 24 indicators.

Successful organisations are recognised for a period of three years, after which time resubmission is necessary. Those recognised are awarded a plaque and are able to use the IIP kitemark on corporate literature. It is usual for the assessor to identify areas for future development, and the expectation is that such improvements will have been made by the time of resubmission for IIP recognition.

CASE STUDY

The selected case study is an example of good practice in the application of TQM principles through the IIP assessment process. In the study school both the deputy headteacher and the head of English recorded and analysed the process (their records were subsequently published: see Thomas 1996 and Hart 1998). The following is a summary of their records.

During 1997–98, Hart and Thomas were involved in the process of submitting an application for reassessment for the IIP standard on behalf of their 11–16 co-educational secondary modern school in the south of England. The school was considered by its staff, pupils and parents to be at the lower end of the league tables. IIP was seen by Thomas as a means of raising standards by developing the school as a learning organisation. The key issues that emerged during this process are outlined under the headings that follow.

Meeting Resistance

Schools are notoriously defensive institutions, and are often sceptical about what they perceive to be the judgements of outsiders. The headteacher drew attention (Thomas 1996) to reasons typically given by schools for resisting the changes required to achieve the IIP standard:

* dissagreement with the assessment that change was really needed together with concern about the possibly deleterious effects of pursuing IIP recognition;
* fear of being required to change too quickly;
* concern over initiative overload and the concomitant loss of quality in teaching and learning.

The implication here is clear: in order to achieve IIP, schools would need to consider the principles of effective TQM (see Chapter 2) – for example, school improvement through staff – rather than regard IIP as an end in itself.

Hart and Thomas found that for IIP to be effective negotiation with staff should include defining role outcomes and identifying training needs to equip them with the skills necessary to fulfil their new roles. Delegation should also be meaningful and productive within the parameters of the staff development plan (SDP) or department development plan (DDP). Further, IIP asserts the importance of communication when working towards meeting objectives, and managers need to look self-critically at their performance in communicating strategy within the school.

This expectation is firmly in line with the TQM principle that managers and their teams play a pivotal role in implementing strategies to meet objectives. Hart found that implementing strategy necessitates the linking of planning at the departmental level to whole-school targets; it also connects with what is arguably the most difficult of Deming's 14 points (see Chapter 2), that of breaking down barriers between departments. If all departments contribute towards whole-school targets, then they share a vision and a purpose.

Appraisal as Part of Training and Development

Training and development is at the heart of IIP and also encompasses several of the five features of TQM identified by Dale and Cooper (1992). In practical terms, appraisal is the key tool in identifying training need and evaluating the effectiveness of the training prescribed, as well as in setting personal targets. This was considered by Hart to be a laudable use of the appraisal process – in TQM terms, moving along the continuum and away from appraisal's function as a measurement of performance towards its becoming a tool for performance delivery. For Sallis (1993: 63)

> the existence of a formal appraisal scheme is an important, though not essential, element in providing evidence that the institution is matching its staff development needs to institutional objectives. IIP can be a potentially useful way of ensuring that appraisals become genuinely developmental tools.

By using appraisal as the primary method of negotiation and discussion with staff, headteachers will need to ensure that the process remains live and therefore relevant to development, and they will probably reap the benefits of appraisal thereby losing its fear-inducing potential. This could lead to the use of appraisals of individual staff to posit more of the issues raised in the public domain. Indeed, this arguably becomes necessary when appraisal is used in this way, for if individual targets are to dovetail with organisational targets, it is difficult to see how total confidentiality can be maintained in the appraisal process. In some instances in the case-study school depart-mental heads moved targets agreed with individuals, including promotional aspirations and individual development, to the DDP.

Alongside this, training which secured for individuals had to be evaluated using a standard approach 'in-house' format, and cascaded to relevant indi-viduals or teams. Consequently, training was made relevant to the school's aims, contributing to a snug interfacing of personal development and school improvement. It is important that staff agree to the passing on of informa-tion and the removal of confidentiality from the appraisal process.

Training

Within the case-study school training came to be perceived, following the more careful management of individuals' training requirements, as more relevant to and focused on the school's needs. As a result of the IIP initiative, training needs were required to be evidenced in training or development plans, or identified through appraisal prior to being funded. In addition, the quality and types of training were perceived to be more congruent to school needs.

The case-study sample indicated also that the application of the IIP principle of investment in individuals appeared to have enhanced motivation among the staff, although there was an acknowledgement that such investment can feel like a personal reward and that this may account for the motivating effect on staff.

Appraisal, training and IIP were perceived to be linked. The appraisal process had not functioned effectively in the study school prior to the inception of IIP assessment. Following its implementation appraisal had come to be considered a positive process. The school found that appraisal could function as a tool in identifying training needs.

The positive impact of IIP on the training-related role of middle managers was acknowledged, as IIP requires that middle managers identify the training needs of their departmental staff, and this they regarded as an empowering function.

IIP was considered to have contributed to the quality of INSET and to the processes in general of staff training and development. IIP was thought to encourage the establishment of TQM principles and practices, for example in the setting up of training structured to improve organisational alignment.

Culture

Not surprisingly, IIP had impacted on the culture of the study school. The IIP standard requires that an organisation considers the effectiveness of its culture. It requires also that structures be established to improve the sharing of organisational aims. Hart found the commitment of staff to IIP culture to be vital to IIP recognition . Knowledge of, and communication about, IIP was perceived as less important than an understanding of the processes, such as appraisal and management responsibility, which are necessary for the successful development of the school's staff. In the case-study school, the IIP assessor identified improved relations with trades union representatives as an issue for development.

IIP was considered to have had an impact on curriculum delivery. Ideally, IIP should contribute to a better-trained and motivated teaching staff, who in turn will impact positively on classroom learning.

A 'hard' edge to IIP was identified by staff involved in pushing through the changes needed to meet the demands of the standard.

The School as a Learning Organisation

Both Thomas and Hart found that staff recognised the benefits of IIP, in particular as a tool useful in school development. The benefits to the organisation are rooted in the submission process. A school which has the IIP standard gains a certain *kudos*, which is attractive to stakeholders. IIP recognition is attractive to applicants because it suggests that their schools hold certain values to be important. While most of these benefits are tangible, many stakeholders would require explanations of them.

Hart commented that the IIP assessment itself had been the most beneficial component, because what had been learned in the process should serve to underpin the continuing work of the school, rather than function just as a finishing touch. The systems the process requires are of more benefit than the IIP logo or kitemark. The process is helpful to schools provided the process is adapted to the needs of the school. The process of triennial resubmission for recognition assists in maintaining such IIP systems as the training plan.

Staff Perceptions of and reactions to IIP

According to Hart teachers believed that IIP recognition offers advantages to the school that it would not otherwise enjoy, though as a measure of a school's quality it was no more highly regarded than the five GCSE A*–C rating. IIP was perceived by some staff as primarily a business standard which demands a change in organisational culture.

Several staff had indicated that, were they to be promoted when applying for a post in another school, they would be likely to encourage IIP there as a tool for school improvement or as a means for self-development. A general response was that there is still some way to go before IIP receives a response of unqualified enthusiasm from teaching staff. The title 'Investors in People' is a statement of value that does not necessarily impinge equally on all staff in the recognised institution, and until the staff as a whole readily perceive that it is being 'invested in' – which is how 'IIP' is often translated – there is likely to be a sceptical response from some or other faction.

IIP School Improvement

Hart considered that perhaps the most important advantage of IIP is that it offers workable boundaries for school improvement. Initial resistance to IIP, according to Thomas, centred on the idea that an off-the-shelf culture audit from the business environment can be readily transferred to measure the culture of service organisations like schools. However, a positive aspect of the business-related culture underpinning IIP is that the process by which the criteria for recognition are met involves keeping operative a clear and meaningful agenda within the organisation. This reduces inertia and keeps the process moving, rather than allowing it to be relegated to the 'back-burner' in deference to the demands of the school's normal operations (Zienau 1996).

Conclusions

A frequent criticism of the IIP standard is that it is a decontextualised and artificial measure against which organisations are required to evaluate their performance. Nevertheless, the standard can contribute towards the process by which an organisation transforms an outdated 'culture-in-use' into a preferred culture which better serves the interests of the school (Egan 1994). As Thomas observed, 'IIP can also provide a tangible management framework to spell out and communicate to all the constituent parts of the "preferred culture"' (1996: 44).

The process of working towards the achievement of the national standard does not of itself ensure improvement in schools' staff management and development systems. However, the indicators force schools to address the training needs and the professional and career development of staff and encourage managers – at all levels – to address the issues which reflect motivation and performance (Zienau 1996). Nevertheless, the management of such issues is dependent upon the ability of the school to implement a cultural shift that places such development at the centre of IIP processes.

While IIP helps to define effective management practice, and through site visits verifies that the indicators are met in reality rather than simply existing as paper systems, managers still have implementation problems to address – including the area of organisational culture – in order to ensure IIP's continuing relevance to schools.

More generally, IIP acts as a stimulus to clarify the basic managerial values a school has or wishes to adopt, and assists in bringing pedagogic and managerial values into closer alignment. Furthermore, a focus on the criteria manifested in the indicators ensures that 'gap analysis' (which reveals the distance of the current state from the standard prescribed by the indicators) retains objectivity and a focus on the school's functions and needs.

Hart found that consultants emphasised the importance of synergy between school improvement and working towards IIP recognition. Thomas believes that IIP is more likely to be accepted by staff if there is a clear link between the initiative and the improvement of teaching and learning, and this is borne out by the case study. IIP, then, is 'potentially a key element in quality management in schools', and a 'culture-change' monitoring and evaluation tool. Adams (1996) argues that there must be linkage of

> an individual's efforts to the achievement of the employing organisation's goals, directly and unequivocally. Through this link all development issues become mainstream managerial concerns which reflect good practice that can be found in some educational organisations ... it reinforces the exhortations that Staff Development and Human Resource Management practitioners make in many organi-

sations about needs, funding, commitment, participation in developmental activities and evaluation.

The case-study school found that IIP offers a cycle of systematic and regular improvement, and, given the demise of GEST budgets, offers a helpful alternative system of development, especially as the standard is reassessed every three years. Cheeseman (1997) offers a personal perspective on the process of the revalidation, in which attention is drawn to the high standards expected of resubmissions. It is insufficient to assume that the previous submission can form the backbone of the resubmission, as evidence of continued improvement in specified areas is required.

Submission for IIP requires a commitment to continuous quality improvement and assurance. Given the nature of the specific targets involved, the assessment process allows 'step-by-step' incremental changes (Brown and Taylor 1996) which

> can be implemented effectively by focusing on minimal, concrete goals ... rather than promoting vast and vague targets with whose desirability nobody would take issue, but whose attainability is another matter altogether.

The need to resubmit triennially for IIP means innovation and improvement can become a cultural norm within the institution, which, provided it is well-managed, is a force for the good. School improvement will not be achieved overnight (OfSTED 1994), but if schools embark on the achievement of the Investors' standard the very process of so doing will ensure that many of the mechanisms and practices necessary to continuous school improvement and effectiveness are put into place (Adams 1996).

To view IIP as a quick and easy route towards school improvement is, however, to misunderstand its principles. Given their genuine commitment to IIP, schools can use its framework to improve their training and development practices. Schools' service-orientation means that the impact of IIP is potentially wide, ranging from the expected impact in improved training and development to organisational synergy and culture. Whether or not it contributes to improved pupil achievement is a matter which this case study has not addressed. Although a 'flow-through' from enhanced and more focused training provision to improved classroom practice and curriculum delivery is to be expected, until a more direct link can be found between IIP and improved pupil achievement scepticism on this matter is unlikely to decline. IIP relies on stakeholders to 'invest' in it in order for its potential to be fully realised.

THE FUTURE

The government intends to continue to encourage schools to become Investors in People (Sebba 1999), as it is an important way of helping them address the training and development needs of all staff. Schools are more likely to succeed when every member of staff, regardless of role, understands what the school is seeking to achieve and what each can do to contribute. Each staff member should have a plan for training and development and be involved in the development of school policies. In practical terms, this would mean, for example, involving teaching assistants, including those who are part-time, in the school's training days and looking imaginatively at ways of developing the role of clerical and administrative staff, and of caretakers, technicians and other support staff, so that the whole school community works together to raise standards. The new category of governor for support staff, which the government has already put in place, will help to drive this message home.

SUMMARY

This chapter has considered the application of TQM principles in a learning organisation through an examination of the process of assessment required for IIP recognition. The IIP standard aims to help organisations and institutions of all kinds to improve their performance and effectiveness by realising the full potential of their workforce. The sector of fastest growth in the take-up of IIP is currently that of schools. It is recognised that the IIP standard contributes the best business practice combining to inform staff development.

IIP demands that the school has a written training and development plan which identifies the training needs of the school's staff and the actions to meet them. IIP also requires the setting of targets for training and development at all levels of the school. Significant, too, is the clear expectation that employees be involved in setting their own training targets.

The case-study school is illustrative of good practice in the application of TQM principles through the IIP assessment process. IIP was considered by the school's leadership to encourage TQM principles and practices, for example the setting up of structures to improve organisational alignment and the provision of training to benefit the organisation. The process of working towards IIP recognition does not of itself ensure improvement in schools' staff management and development systems. Nevertheless, the indicators force schools to address the training requirements and the professional and career development of their staff; and they encourages managers – at all levels – to address the issues which reflect motivation and performance.

The government will continue to encourage schools to become Investors in People, which is an important way of helping them address the training and development needs of all staff. Schools are more likely to succeed when every member of staff, regardless of their role, understands what the school is seeking to achieve and what they can do to contribute.

This chapter concludes Part I and the focus on theoretical issues. Part II presents a summary of recent government policies relating to the management of professional development in schools.

Part II

THE NATIONAL CONTEXT

As Part I demonstrated, total quality management theory and practice focuses on the needs of employees and customers within an organisation. Effective professional development policies will reflect these needs and contribute to the organisation's ability to improve and move forward. A learning organisation is a moving organisation, one that values employees and customers.

It is government policies that create legislation and the parameters for maintained schools. In the 1990s, consecutive governments have stated that raising standards in schools is a necessity, and there has been much research and policy writing in this area. Significantly, policies have related to training across the board, from qualified teacher status through to school leadership. Practitioners are required to meet targets that are set within the legislative framework, and this endeavour has been supported by DfEE funding for professional development.

Part II provides an overview of the government's most recent initiatives for the professional development of teachers. These include the national standards for teachers, the Advanced Skills Teacher grade, leadership programmes for aspirant headteachers, and for new and serving headteachers, and the Standards Fund for the in-service training of teachers. Each Chapter in Part II provides evidence that the establishing of a continuous professional development programme will be a core activity for teachers. The challenge is to relate this to schools as learning organisations.

Chapter 4 presents a digest of current government policies and initiatives developed by the Department for Education and Employment (DfEE) and the Teacher Training Agency (TTA). The *National Standards for Teachers* (TTA 1998e) emphasise the government's drive to raise standards in schools through a number of initiatives, including the professional development of teachers. The delicate balance that exists between the weight of government policy and the drive by schools towards learning organisation status is illustrated. As in other areas of education, such governmental initiatives have the potential to either enhance or suppress teachers' motivation to embrace professional development in schools.

Chapter 5 describes government legislation and guidance for the training of qualified teachers. Consideration is given to how schools as learning organisations might embrace initial teacher training. The issue of partnerships with higher education institutions (HEIs), designed to enhance practice and develop the principle of continuous professional development for staff, trainee teacher and school leader alike, is also considered.

Chapter 6 examines government initiatives for the induction and development of classroom teachers, Career Entry Profiles and the Advanced Skills Teacher scheme.

Part II concludes with an evaluation, in Chapter 7, of the TTA's training programmes for headteachers: the National Professional Qualification for Headteachers (NPQH); the Headteacher Leadership and Management Programme (HEADLAMP) and the Leadership Programme for Serving Headteachers (LPSH). Each evaluation considers the impact of training on participants, schools and the development of learning organisations.

INTRODUCTION

The government has provided a framework which aims to raise standards in schools through the enhancement of professional practice. The *National Standards for Teachers* (TTA 1998e) is an example of policy in practice through the TTA's identification of competences required at different levels of the profession. The TTA has produced a checklist of effective practice extending through from initial teacher education to school leadership. This identification of competences is supported by training opportunities that are compulsory for trainee and newly qualified teachers, and reccommended for subject leaders, special educational needs' co-ordinators, and headteachers (although the NPQH will become compulsory in 2002). Government guidance and legislation has also provided teachers with the option to remain in the classroom as Advanced Skills Teachers.

The effectiveness of government policy has yet to be determined. Evaluations by participants have indicated a mixed response, and the prescriptive nature of initial teacher education has been criticised by the Universities Council for the Education of Teachers (UCET) (Wilkin1998). The introduction of the NPQH, HEADLAMP and LPSH programmes is to be welcomed; however, the impact of these programmes on school effectiveness is difficult to assess.The NPQH's content is presented to participants in a corporate style. The TTA appears to have moved away from the core purpose of managing schools: learning and teaching. This has been recognised (see Green 1999) and will be addressed by the TTA and DfEE in due course. A litmus-test of the impact of the NPQH, in particular, will be the approach taken by governors to the appointment to headships of NPQH award-holders.

The development of appraisal is also to be welcomed (Part III) as schools have experienced difficulty with this area of the management of professional development. The relationship of appraisal to Career Entry Profiles and induction requires further clarification and development.

In short, the essence of the problem of managing the implementation of government initiatives is the co-ordination and recording of individual training opportunities within the school context. The professional development co-ordinator and the senior managers require information on all training and development opportunities available for their staff. A possible solution could be the introduction of profiles for teachers, extending from appointment to transfer to another position or through to retirement. Relevant documentation might include:

1   career entry profile
2   induction profile
3   record of INSET
4   record of training participation and any awards
5   summary documents – appraisal
6   career targets
7   school targets – as stated in the school development plan
8   curriculum vitae
9   job description.

A 'career profile' would provide supporting evidence for teachers when applying for internal or external posts, or for courses. Whatever the system, the importance of the training process is paramount, as is the relevance of training to practice.

4

GOVERNMENT POLICY

INTRODUCTION

Maintained schools function under the auspices of central government policy it is through the effective management of professional development in schools that government intends to achieve two aims: raising achievement and the encouragement of lifelong learning. The present government, determined to raise standards in English schools, has focused attention, in turn, on target setting, literacy and numeracy, and, more recently, the professional development of teachers. Following the report *Lifelong Learning* (NAGCELL 1997), the government has emphasised the importance of the development of learning organisations in the workplace. Schools are considered to be central to this initiative.

This chapter provides an introduction to government policies and practices on professional development, beginning with a consideration of the Teacher Training Agency (TTA) and the National Standards for Teachers. Funding and inspection arrangements are also considered, and the chapter concludes with a summary of key themes emerging from the Green Paper (DfEE 1998d).

BACKGROUND TO THE GOVERNMENT'S PROFESSIONAL DEVELOPMENT POLICIES

This section provides a description of some of the diverse professional development opportunities available over the last fifteen years. Until 1987, the professional development of teachers focused on award-bearing courses although provision did also extend to short courses and training for specific needs (Gaunt 1995). Significant changes in provision for the professional development of teachers occurred in 1985, and the resulting policies impact on current practice. The White Paper *Better Schools* (DES 1985) asserted that existing INSET resources were not effective, and that shorter, less traditional, activities would be more appropriate than the longer higher education courses.

Teachers were able to access such courses from several sources including LEAs, higher education institutes and consultants. LEAs established subject-specific or management-related training groups, and such practice continues today. Professional development was to relate directly to practice, the improvement of teaching and learning and classroom management and assessment. Funding was available for teachers to be trained in matters specific to practice.

The DfEE-funded Grants for Education Support and Training (GEST) enabled LEAs to provide training either by using their own staff or to buy-in expertise from higher education (HE) or the growing number of private trainers. GEST funds also provided the means for purchasing materials and equipment, the employment of advisory teachers and the training of non-teaching staff and governors (Gaunt 1995). The funding process presented headteachers with the opportunity to collaborate with LEA support staff on the development of INSET programmes. With the emphasis on practitioner training, the GEST initiative provided a framework for whole-school staff development. The broad scope of GEST funding accommodated a range of INSET programmes. This changed in 1997 with the introduction of the Standards Fund, which, since then, has provided the resources for government-initiated professional development. Schools and LEAs now are encouraged to bid for the funding for professional development, and selection is by the DfEE.

Figure 4.1 summarises the emergence and evolution of professional development in schools. It indicates that government involvement in the professional development of teachers has increased over time. The provision is now more structured and related to government policies and targets. This is further illustrated by the funding mechanisms. The responsibility for the provision of government-funded training and development opportunities for teachers has transferred from LEAs to the DfEE and the Teacher Training Agency (TTA). Whether standards in schools are rising as a result of these initiatives has yet to be assessed. Evaluations of leadership programmes focusing on management and delivery have been published (see Chapter 7), but there have been no published assessments of the impact of the schemes on the standards in schools.

As stated in Chapter 1, the number of professional development opportunities for school staff is increasing. If such opportunities are to relate effectively to practice they will need to be managed in conjunction with school-based LEA and HE provision. Practitioners and managers will need to be aware of the range of available internal and external programmes and of the guidance on how to relate these to practice.

The current initiatives directed by the government through the TTA are managed and delivered by regional centres. These include:

- the *National Standards for Teachers* (TTA 1998e), comprising Qualified Teacher Status (QTS), the National Professional Qualification for

Subject Leaders (NPQSL), the National Professional Qualification for Special Educational Needs Coordinators (SENCO);

• the National Professional Qualification for Headteachers (NPQH), the Headteacher Leadership and Management Programme (HEADLAMP) and induction programmes.

In this context, the TTA acts as maker and implementer of policy, and, with the Office for Standards in Education (OfSTED), inspector of provision.

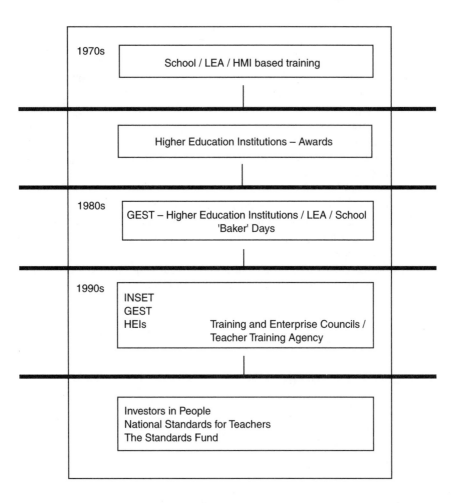

1970s	School / LEA / HMI based training
	Higher Education Institutions – Awards
1980s	GEST – Higher Education Institutions / LEA / School 'Baker' Days
1990s	INSET GEST HEIs — Training and Enterprise Councils / Teacher Training Agency
	Investors in People National Standards for Teachers The Standards Fund

Figure 4.1 The emergence of professional development for teachers

TEACHING TRAINING AGENCY

The TTA was established by the government in 1994 to review and develop the training of teachers. Central to the TTA's concerns is school effectiveness, set within the context of the government's school improvement programme. The stated purpose of the TTA is to raise standards in schools by improving the quality of school leadership, teaching and teacher-training, and by raising the status and self-esteem of the teaching profession. This has led to the creation of a range of initiatives focusing on improving training and development opportunities for teachers in schools. The emphasis is on good teaching, and, as the TTA's chief executive Anthea Millett commented at the first TTA Annual Lecture, 'good teaching is what makes a difference to children's learning' (1996a: 18).

In 1995, the TTA commissioned MORI to survey teachers on the value and effectiveness of INSET programmes. The results were disappointing. While INSET represented a huge investment nationally of around £400 million per annum, teachers were less than enthusiastic about the efficacy of existing programmes for improving their practice. In response, the TTA developed a structure of national standards for teachers in order to promote well-targeted, effective and co-ordinated continuing professional development. The national standards framework is designed to:

- establish clear and explicit expectations of teachers;
- help set targets for professional development and career progression;
- help to focus and improve training and staff development at national, local and school levels;
- ensure that the focus at every point is on improving pupil achievement;
- recognise the expertise required of effective headteachers and teachers in schools.

It is intended that the national standards will provide a focus for professional development for

- newly qualified teachers
- Advanced Skills Teachers
- subject leaders – NPQSL
- special needs' co-ordinators – SENCO
- aspiring headteachers – NPQH
- serving headteachers – HEADLAMP

Stages of Development

The TTA considers that professional development builds on initial teacher training (ITT) and induction, and encompasses the educational, developmental and training opportunities that are present throughout a teacher's career (Green 1999). Figure 4.2 illustrates the stages of development in relation to a teacher's career as reflected in the Teacher Training Agency's national standards' framework (TTA 1998e) and government initiatives.

Figure 4.2 indicates that the stages of a teacher's career can be considered in terms of classroom-teacher and management opportunities. These are described in more detail later in this section. The reader should recognise that these stages reflect the importance for *all* staff within a learning organisation

TTA National Standard/Government Initiative	Stage of Career
Initial Teacher Training	Trainee - Career Entry Profile
Qualified Teacher Status Induction	Practitioner
Advanced Skills Teacher	Expert Classroom Practitioner
National Standards for Subject Leaders	Head of Department Key-Stage Co-ordinator Subject Co-ordinator Head of Year
National Standards for Special Educational Needs Co-ordinators	Head of Special Educational Needs
National Standards for Headteachers	Deputy Headteacher/ Aspiring Headteacher
Headteachers' Management and Leadership Programme	Newly Appointed Headteacher
Leadership Programme for Serving Headteachers	Serving Headteacher

Figure 4.2   TTA national standards in relation to positions of responsibility in schools

of participating in such training and development. The DfEE and TTA appear to have acknowledged that the individual's choice to pursue a managerial career or to extend his or her teaching career should not restrict his or her professional development opportunities. Indeed, it is now recognised that effective classroom teachers should be encouraged to remain in the classroom and to assist others in improving their practice.

The TTA, through the national standards' framework, has grasped the nettle of professional development for teachers. The challenge to all educationalists is how to relate the new initiatives to existing provision and school improvement. Teachers are to be encouraged to put their confidence in the process, while leaders need to develop their knowledge and skills in order to manage the impact of the national standards on their schools.

NATIONAL STANDARDS

Qualified Teacher Status

The TTA through the DfEE's Circular 4/98 (1998a) produced regulations for all newly qualified teachers, the main foci of which are knowledge of and ability to teach the National Curriculum. In addition, newly qualified teachers require planning, teaching and class-management skills. The standards for the award of Qualified Teacher Status (QTS) are based on:

- knowledge and understanding;
- planning, teaching and classroom management;
- monitoring, assessment, recording, reporting and accountability.

Circular 4/98 requires that newly qualified teachers demonstrate the ability to plan their teaching so that it facilitates pupils' progression in learning. This ability is indicated by:

- identifying clear teaching objectives and content;
- setting tasks which challenge and interest pupils;
- setting appropriately demanding expectations;
- setting clear targets for pupils' learning, building on prior attainment;
- identifying pupils' needs;
- making effective use of assessment information;
- planning learning opportunities which contribute to the personal, spiritual, moral, social and cultural development of pupils.

In the context of teaching and class management, the TTA requires newly qualified teachers to:

- ensure effective teaching of whole classes, groups and individuals;
- monitor and intervene when teaching to ensure sound learning and discipline;
- establish a safe learning environment;
- use teaching methods which sustain the momentum of pupils' work and engage all pupils;
- be familiar with the code of practice on special educational needs;
- ensure that pupils acquire and consolidate knowledge, skills and understanding in the subject.

Partnership issues relating to the initial training of teachers in schools are considered in Chapter 5.

Subject Leaders

The national standards for subject leaders (TTA 1998e) set out the knowledge, understanding, skills and attributes that relate to subject leadership, define expertise in subject leadership and guide the professional development of teachers aiming to increase their effectiveness as subject leaders or of those aspiring to take responsibility for leading a subject.

While standards apply to all schools, the TTA emphasises the need to apply and implement standards differently in schools of different type, size or phase. For example, they should be used selectively in smaller primary schools where headteachers may retain more of their defined roles than is the case in larger primary schools. The extent to which subject co-ordinators in primary and special schools can use their knowledge, understanding, skills and attributes in order to carry out the key tasks specified in these standards will depend on their experience and the opportunities to develop their role. The subject leader standards are based on the practices of experienced and effective co-ordinators in providing leadership in their subject(s). The standards are in five parts:

1   core purpose of subject leadership
2   key outcomes of subject leadership
3   professional knowledge and understanding
4   skills and attributes
5   key areas of subject leadership.

Although subject leaders are expected to have a good grasp of their subject and to be able to lead by example through the quality of their own teaching, standards focus primarily on expertise in leadership and management of subjects. While some aspects of leadership and management are generic, others are specific to particular subjects, and also to types of school. It is intended that training and development for subject leadership will provide a good grounding in many of the leadership and management skills necessary to take on broad and more senior management roles.

The national standards for subject leaders form the basis of the National Professional Qualification for Subject Leaders (NPQSL). The NPQSL is yet to be implemented; further developments are underway, and the TTA intends to launch the training scheme in the near future. The development of the NPQSL reflects awareness of the need for a clearer understanding of middle management issues (an examination of aspects of the middle management of schools is given in Chapter 10).

Special Educational Needs' Co-ordinators

The TTA considers that SENCOs will need to develop the particular aspects of knowledge and understanding required for co-ordinating SEN in a school. These have been developed as a qualification within the *National Standards for Teachers* (TTA 1998e). These standards are in five parts:

1 core purpose of the SENCO
2 key outcomes of SEN co-ordination
3 professional knowledge and understanding
4 skills and attributes
5 key areas of SEN co-ordination.

The TTA acknowledges that the depth of knowledge required in any aspect will vary according to the range of needs of the pupils in specific schools; the TTA also emphasises the importance of SENCOs remaining up to date with developments – in special education in particular and in education generally.

The standards state that, in order to be effective, SENCOs require the ability to communicate with clarity and the disposition to listen to and take account of the views of others. They should also have skills of self-management and time management.

The TTA recognises that the attributes required of SENCOs are generally those required of all teachers who are successful and effective in their leadership and management roles. SENCOs co-ordinate, with the support of the headteacher and within the context of the school's aims and policies, the development and implementation of the SEN policy in order to improve the quality of education provided and so raise pupils' standards of achievement.

The standards require SENCOs to seek to develop, with the support of the headteacher and colleagues, practices that are effective in overcoming barriers to learning, and to sustain effective teaching through the analysis and assessment of pupils' needs: monitoring both the quality of the teaching and the standards achieved by pupils, and the setting of appropriate improvement targets. With support from the headteacher and governing body, SENCOs identify resources appropriate to support the teaching of pupils with special educational needs, and monitor their use in terms of efficiency, effectiveness and safety.

The TTA expects the effective co-ordination of SEN to have a range of practical outcomes, including:

1   *Pupils* on the SEN register who are

- progressing towards the targets set in their individual education plans;
- showing improved in literacy, numeracy and IT skills;
- being assisted to access the wider curriculum;
- motivated to learn and to develop self-esteem and confidence in their ability as learners.

2   *Teachers* who

- capably implement the school's SEN policy and practice in meeting the needs of pupils;
- identify pupils who may require special provision, e.g. those with educational and behavioural difficulties (EBD), and help to prepare individual education plans as appropriate;
- communicate effectively with the parents, the SENCO and all other staff with responsibilities for SEN, including those from external agencies;
- have high expectations of pupils' progress, set realistic but challenging targets which they monitor and review, and in relation to which they provide the appropriate support.

3   *Learning support assistants* who

- understand their role in the school in relation to pupils with SEN;
- work collaboratively with the SENCO, with teaching staff and staff from external agencies;
- develop their skills and extend their understanding, through training and development, the better to assist pupils in maximising their levels of achievement and independence.

4   *Headteachers and senior managers* who

- recognise that the curriculum must be relevant to all pupils by taking SEN into account in the formulation and implementation of policies throughout the school;

- understand how best to support those with responsibility for SEN co-ordination.

5 *Parents* who

- understand the targets set for their children and willingly help their children work towards them;
- become fully involved as partners in the education process.

The national standards have been developed into the National Professional Qualification for Special Educational Needs' Co-ordinators. The effectiveness of the standards and the qualification in terms of professional development and impact on practice has yet to be measured.

Aspirant Headteachers

In 1997, the TTA developed a scheme for the training of aspiring head-teachers called the National Professional Qualification for Headship. The NPQH is to become a prerequisite for headteachers in 2002. NPQH courses to meet the requirements of the national standards for headteachers (TTA 1998e) are delivered on a modular basis, covering:

1 core purpose of the headteacher
2 key outcomes of headship
3 professional knowledge and understanding
4 skills and attributes
5 key areas of headship

Training is delivered across the country at ten Regional Training and Development Centres. Trainers have been selected from the ranks of retired and practising headteachers, HEI lecturers and LEA advisers. Funding is allocated by the TTA to aspiring headteachers through a selection process administered by an applicant's LEA and/or the TTA. The NPQH sets out the knowledge, understanding, skills and attributes that relate to the key areas of headship, in particular leadership and management which ensure high-quality teaching and learning and lead to raised standards of achieve-ment.

The NPQH aims to be a high-quality national professional qualification which:

- draws on the best management practice inside and outside education;
- provides an assurance to governors and others that newly appointed NPQH holders have the foundations of school leadership and manage-

ment knowledge, and the understanding and skills necessary to perform successfully against national standard criteria;

- is sufficiently rigorous to ensure that only those fitted for headship gain the qualification, while having the flexibility to take account of candidates' existing skills and prior achievements;
- incorporates indicators to help headteachers, governors and LEAs evaluate candidates' potential to gain the qualification;
- enables a recently appointed headteacher, in the context of the new school, to extend the aquired leadership and management abilities by progressing to HEADLAMP, the development programme for new headteachers.

The first cohort to achieve the NPQH took up headteacher posts in 1998–99. An evaluation of the NPQH is given in Chapter 7.

HEADLAMP

The programme for new headteachers, the first of the leadership initiatives to be introduced, differs from the qualifications based on the national standards in terms both of its aims and its mode of delivery. The selection and funding of incumbent headteachers for professional development through HEADLAMP are matters decided by governing bodies and the headteachers themselves rather than by LEAs. All first-headship appointees are entitled to a grant of £2,500 from the DfEE, via the TTA, this sum to be paid in return for training received from HEADLAMP providers within two years of their appointment. The choice is wide: currently the list of registered HEAD-LAMP providers has 198 entries, and these include HEIs, organisations such as Gallup and Relate, independent companies and partnerships, individual consultants and some, but not all, LEAs.

A detailed evaluation of HEADLAMP is given in Chapter 8.

Leadership Programme for Serving Headteachers

The national standards for the LPSH (TTA 1998d) set out in five areas the knowledge, understanding, skills and abilities which relate to key tasks of headship:

1 strategic direction and development of the school
2 learning and teaching
3 people and relationships
4 development and deployment of people and resources
5 accountability for the efficiency and effectiveness of the school.

The standards are designed to serve as focal points for the training and development of serving headteachers. The purpose of the programme is to secure for all participants further improvements in their leadership in order to improve the quality of education and standards of achievement in their schools. The programme recognises that headteachers start from positions of strength and can demonstrate considerable expertise, knowledge, understanding and skills in school leadership and management. The TTA states that relevant professional development of the highest quality will therefore be on offer, focusing on the individual needs of each participant within a high status national programme.

With its focus on the link between the personal effectiveness of head-teachers and school improvement (the 'how' as well as the 'what' of headship), the programme is intended to be challenging. The LPSH has been designed to complement other professional development opportunities for serving headteachers. The programme

- is underpinned by the national standards for headteachers and by evidence from interviews with highly effective headteachers;
- institutes at the outset a thorough analysis and evaluation of personal and school performance, providing a sharp focus for subsequent training and development;
- contains a structured four-day residential workshop, and continuing professional development and support;
- makes direct links between the headteacher's personal targets and the school's targets for raising pupils' achievement;
- is a confidential process which combines challenge and support in a setting which provides space for critical analysis;
- offers participants the opportunity, on neutral territory, to work along-side other headteachers from different types of school and parts of the UK, so enabling the sharing of expertise outside of their local networks.

Further discussion of the LPSH can be found in Chapter 7.

FUNDING

In addition to individual grants allocated by LEAs and the TTA for training in fulfilment of the national standards for teachers, the government has developed the following mechanism for funding professional development in schools:

The Standards Fund

The Standards Fund (DfEE 1997b) makes available a range of grants to schools, LEAs and other agencies for professional development opportunities that focus on the government's central priority of raising standards as set out in the White Paper *Excellence in Schools* (DfEE 1997a). The fund is for training related to school self-improvement in order to meet targets agreed with LEAs as stated in school and LEA development plans. It is the role of LEAs to support schools in this process.

The government considers that schools are best placed, in most cases, to identify their own development needs and priorities, and therefore a large proportion of the Standards Fund is devolved to schools themselves. But LEAs also have an important role in supporting schools in raising standards. From 1998, LEA targets and priorities have been presented in individual education development plans (EDPs). The government advises that LEAs will need to take account of EDPs and any preliminary planning it has done in making decisions regarding the distribution of devolved funds to schools and, where devolution is not appropriate, decisions on the expenditure of some grants.

The government states that activities funded through the Standards Fund are not to replicate or replace those separately funded from other LEA resources or other government grants, such as the single regeneration budget (SRB) or projects involving Training and Enterprise Councils (TECs) and private finance. What the Standards Fund underwrites is required to be additional to, coherent with, and mutually reinforcing of related activities funded through other sources.

In focusing on the raising of standards and school self-improvement, the Standards Fund continues to reflect the national priorities for teachers' professional development identified by the TTA. It is important that support for teachers' professional development is sufficiently targeted to meet the needs of teachers and their pupils. A number of key elements and principles should underpin professional development in order to increase teachers' effectiveness, ensure school improvement, and raise pupils' standards of achievement. The government requires LEAs and schools to ensure:

- proper targeting of development opportunities through needs' assessment and appraisal;
- rigorous quality assurance of provision so that professional development activities address identified needs;
- effective monitoring and evaluation of development activities and the setting of targets for improvement for the maximum impact of professional development on classroom practice;
- that the (annual) five non-contact days are used as part of schools' planned programmes of professional development;
- accountability to school governors for the professional development of staff and its impact.

A summary of the Standards Fund allocations to LEAs in 1998–99 is given in Table 4.1:

Table 4.1   The Standards Fund: summary of bids 1998–99

Grants 1–20	Formula or Competitive	Grant rate
1 School effectiveness	Formula	50
2 School leadership	Formula	50–100
3 Newly qualified teachers	Formula	50
4 Early Years' training and development	Formula	50
5 Reduction of infant class size	Formula	100
6 Assessment	Formula	50
7 National literacy strategy: primary	Competitive	50
8 National literacy project: KS 3	Competitive	50
9 Literacy summer schools	Competitive	50
10 Family literacy	Competitive	50
11 Premier league club study support centre	–	50
12 Special Educational Needs	Semi-competitive	50
13 Qualifications	Formula	50
14 Work-related learning	Competitive	50
15 Attendance and behaviour	Competitive	50
16 Drug prevention	Formula	50
17 Youth service	Formula	50
18 School security	Formula	75
19 Specialist schools	Formula	100
20 Specialist-teacher assistants	–	80

OFFICE FOR STANDARDS IN EDUCATION (OFSTED)

A final consideration pertinent to the relationship between professional development and legislation is *inspection*. OfSTED recognises the importance of professional development at all levels, and its inspectors are required to evaluate professional development during the school inspection process.

Inspectors must also evaluate and report on the adequacy of staffing. Their judgements are based on the extent to which

- the number, qualifications and experience of teachers and other class-room staff match the demands of the curriculum;
- arrangements for the induction, appraisal and professional development of staff contribute to their effectiveness.

The inspection report evaluates whether the school is staffed and resourced to teach the curriculum effectively, and whether there are any features which clearly contribute to or detract from quality and standards. A key question is:

Do the number, qualifications and experience of teachers and other classroom staff match the demands of the curriculum?

The staff as a whole should have sufficient knowledge and expertise to meet the requirements of the school's curriculum. Inspectors assess the extent to which the level of staffing enables the effective teaching of the curriculum to all pupils. Inspectors also consider whether there are enough appropriately skilled support staff to enable the teaching, administration and day-to-day life of the school to function effectively, and the extent to which classroom assistants work with teachers in planning, teaching and recording pupils' progress. A summary is presented in Figure 4.3.

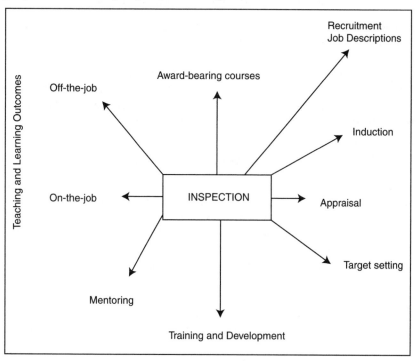

Figure 4.3   OfSTED inspection and professional development

THE FUTURE

In December 1998 the government published a Green Paper (DfEE 1998b) and, early the following year, a supporting Technical Paper (DfEE 1999) which include guidance on the initial and continuing development of teachers. The proposals are summarised in what follows.

Support for New Teachers

The Green Paper (DfEE 1998b) states that professional development starts when a new teacher first enters school. The government proposes that from September 1999 there will be a statutory induction year for those coming new to teaching. The starting-point for the induction will be the Career Entry Profile, which identifies the strengths of each newly trained teacher and his or her priorities for professional development. The government intends to provide the necessary funding to guarantee all new teachers a reduced teaching load and a programme of support to ensure that they have the time to consolidate and improve their performance.

Career and Professional Development

The government believes that a firm career-long commitment to professional development should be at the heart of every teacher's professionalism, and is therefore investing in teachers' professional development through the Standards Fund to support national training priorities such as literacy, numeracy and school improvement. In addition, the New Opportunities Fund, introduced in late 1999, will provide £230 million across the UK to ensure that teachers become confident in the use of ICT in subject teaching.

A New Training Framework

To formalise the importance of career and professional development the government proposes that teachers' contracts of employment will include a duty to keep their skills up-to-date, and it is expected that this updating of skills will be reflected in teachers' personal and career development targets which will be agreed as part of the annual appraisal process. Further, the government considers that there are three distinct, and equally important, elements to be taken into account:

1   *national* training priorities focused on particular needs which have been identified nationally, e.g. literacy, numeracy, ICT, headship training, special educational needs;

2   *school* priorities emerging from development planning to help schools reach their own targets and implement their post-OfSTED action plans; and

3   *individual* development needs of teachers identified through annual appraisal.

Monitoring Quality

The government believes that new quality assurance arrangements are needed so that schools and teachers can be confident that training time and money are invested in good quality provision. The government will consult on a new national Code of Practice, aimed at all major providers of publicly funded training, which is expected, for example, to require providers to reflect up-to-date research and inspection evidence, to link provision directly to the proposed new career structure, and to include mechanisms for monitoring and evaluating the impact on pupil performance.

The General Teaching Council (GTC)

In addition to a legislative framework for the training of teachers the government intends to create a General Teaching Council (GTC). As the new professional body for teachers, the GTC will have a key interest in both teaching standards and professional development. Once the GTC is fully established, the government will expect it to consider how the Green Paper's proposals might be reflected. A Code of Practice will be issued to lay down standards of professional conduct and practice expected of registered teachers. The government advises that the GTC may wish to consider whether there should be a professional duty for teachers to keep their skills up to date which would underpin the new contractual duty. It may want to consider also how teachers' achievements against the new career framework are to be recorded on the new national register of teachers.

The government has stated that teachers will make up a majority of the GTC's membership, which will also include people appointed by major representative bodies in education and by the Secretary of State. The government proposes that the GTC will

*   prepare the Code of Practice laying down the standards of professional conduct and practice expected of registered teachers;
*   maintain a register of qualified teachers – teachers in maintained schools will be required to register, paying a modest annual fee;
*   have the power to strike off from its register any teacher deemed to have engaged in professionally unacceptable conduct or to be incompetent; the GTC will advise the Secretary of State on misconduct cases which arise from child protection concerns;

- hear any appeals against LEA decisions that newly qualified teachers had failed their induction year;
- advise the Secretary of State and others on a wide range of teaching issues: from recruitment and supply, through training and induction, to professional development and conduct. The GTC will have a major role to play in advising on teacher training, and the Secretary of State will be required to consult the GTC on any future change in standards required for entry to the profession.

The government proposes that GTC will be an authoritative professional voice which will give teachers the means by which to regulate their profession and influence the way it develops. It is the government's intention that the Council will be established by 2000.

Higher Education

The government recognises that many teachers also make a significant investment in their own personal development, for example by taking post-graduate courses leading to awards at Masters or Doctorate levels. Within the new career structure, the government will expect to see teachers contributing to the training cost of such personal development initiatives, particularly once they are above the performance threshold. The government intends to offer additional support to those who are at the start of their careers or on lower earnings. The government also intends to pilot, in the year 2000, new opportunities for using Individual Learning Accounts to encourage the professional development of teachers, classroom assistants and support staff.

SUMMARY

This chapter has shown that it is through the effective management of professional development that the government intends to promote two aims: raising achievement and lifelong learning. Current government initiatives include those directed by the TTA, and managed and delivered by regional centres, including the national standards and qualifications for teachers: Qualified Teacher Status (QTS); National Professional Qualification for Subject Leaders (NPQSL); National Professional Qualification for Special Education Needs Co-ordinators (NPQSENCO); National Professional Qualification for Headteachers (NPQH); Headteachers Leadership and Management Programme (HEADLAMP); Leadership Programme for Serving Headteachers and induction programmes.

The government recognises that many teachers will also make a significant investment in their own personal development, for example by taking post-graduate degrees.

A more detailed analysis follows of the professional development opportunities available to practitioners within the government's national standards framework.

5

INITIAL TEACHER TRAINING

INTRODUCTION

The previous chapter introduced the government's requirements for newly qualified teachers within the context of the *National Standards for Teachers* (TTA 1998e). This chapter considers the practical implications of the standards as presented in Circular 4/98 (DfEE 1998a), in particular the development of school partnerships and the role of school mentors in initial teacher training (ITT). It also considers the importance of the partnership between higher education institutions (HEIs) and schools in the development of schools as learning organisations.

QUALIFIED TEACHER STATUS

QTS is a requirement for all those who teach in a maintained school in England and Wales and, as such, represents the first national professional qualification in the government's framework of standards and qualifications for teachers.

QTS is awarded after satisfactory completion of a course of ITT, either concurrently with or after the award of a first degree from a UK or an overseas' university or a HEI with degree-awarding powers. Following Circular 10/97 (DfEE 1997e) and Circular 4/98 (DfEE 1998a) a range of opportunities exists leading to the award of QTS: BEd, BA(QTS), PGCE, the Graduate Teacher Programme, the Registered Teacher Programme, the Licensed Teacher Scheme and the Overseas' Trained Teacher Scheme. Each course can be completed by full-time or part-time study. Students can train on primary (3–11 or 5–11) and secondary (11–16 or 11–18) age ranges.

Successful completion of a course or programme of ITT, including employment-based provision, requires trainees to achieve all of the QTS standards, and all courses assess trainees against the national standards.

The role of HEIs in ITT is changing, with schools now playing a far more active role in the training of teachers. This change has been introduced at a time when HEIs are subject to more intensive control and inspection. Relations with schools are also tightly specified (see Wilkin 1998).

As stated in the previous chapter, newly-qualified teachers are required by the national standards' framework to have thorough knowledge of and ability to teach the National Curriculum, and must possess planning, teaching and class-management skills. In order to achieve QTS, trainees must display competence in tracking pupil progression by

- identifying clear teaching objectives and content;
- setting tasks which challenge and interest pupils;
- setting appropriate and demanding expectations;
- setting clear targets for learning which build on pupils' prior attainment;
- identifying pupils' needs;
- making effective use of assessment information;
- planning opportunities to contribute to pupils' personal, spiritual, moral, social and cultural development.

In the context of teaching and class management, the TTA requires NQTs to demonstrate their ability to

- ensure effective teaching of whole classes, and of groups and individuals;
- monitor and intervene when teaching to ensure sound learning and discipline;
- establish a safe environment;
- use diverse teaching methods to engage the interest of all pupils and sustain the momentum of their work;
- apply the code of practice on special educational needs;
- ensure that pupils acquire and consolidate knowledge, skills and understanding in the subject.

PARTNERSHIP

The professional development of trainee teachers is now firmly rooted in partnerships between local schools and HEIs (DfEE 1998b). As already indicated, ITT programmes are now set within a framework of shared practice that is dependent on mutual respect and understanding. School–HEI partnerships are required to consider whole-school matters, e.g. the management of discipline and organisational issues, when they prepare trainee teachers for professional practice (Bines and Welton 1995). Any involvement in training teachers should be preceded by whole-school consultation, taking into account the views of individual teachers, departments, parents, governors and pupils. A school's priorities, as identified in the school development plan (SDP), should be considered at an early stage, and if it is to become a focus within the school ITT should be integrated with the professional development programme identified in the plan.

For schools intending to enter into a partnership, a cost–benefit analysis of the potential consequences is strongly recommended. The benefits which can accrue from appropriately resourced involvement in ITT include

- the raising of a school's collective self-image by its association with a HEI;
- an enhanced reputation, leading to possible improvements in the recruitment and retention of the school's staff;
- access to the expertise and facilities of higher education;
- greater individual and collective learning for teachers, leading to heightened critical awareness of their practice;
- career development opportunities for teachers who act as professional tutors, or 'mentors', to trainee teachers.

The costs to schools include those of time, resources, teacher expertise and the impact on pupils' learning of an increased focus on the training of teachers. The school is responsible for

- developing consistent and worthwhile programmes for trainees of different ages and stages in their learning and aptitudes;
- the formal assessment and counselling of trainees, including those whose placements are proving unsuccessful;
- providing release time for mentors to support trainees and for their own training needs to be met.

School responsibilities should be considered alongside the more significant issues of funding, potential increases in workload and the implications for pupils' learning. The costs of providing specific support, such as adequate library and ICT facilities for trainees, should also be assessed.

Criteria for Evaluating ITE Courses

Before introducing ITE courses to any school, senior managers and the professional development co-ordinator should consider the value-added benefits to the school. The following may help in this process:

- Trainees must be excluded from the staffing complement of the school.
- Courses should include a HEI course of study.
- Courses should lead to a qualification which is validated by a HEI.
- Courses should provide trainees with significant experience in two or more schools and the opportunity to change school if a teaching practice is not going well. The situation in which a trainee is admitted, educated,

assessed and certificated largely within one school will not lead to an adequate teaching experience covering a sufficiently broad range of pupils' needs.

- Mentors or teacher tutors, with sufficient training, preparation and resources, should be afforded cover and a reduced timetable to allow them to fulfil ITE responsibilities, without additional workload.
- Courses should have guaranteed funding over time and sufficient resources to prevent consequences detrimental to a school's primary responsibility for pupils' learning.
- Courses should focus on child development and learning, educational psychology, special educational needs, the needs of pupils who do not have English or Welsh as a first language, the philosophy and theory of education in general, subject knowledge and practical skills for the classroom.

Balancing Funding with Responsibility

Where an ITE partnership is being negotiated between a school governing body and a HEI, both sides will need to be open and fair about the costs and benefits.

The amount of money per student which schools receive from HEIs will depend on the school's share of responsibility for ITE. The balance of responsibility and, therefore, the amount of funding per trainee given to a school may well vary from one partnership to another.

In any event, the resources made available to the school must be sufficient to

- allow the school's teachers to fulfil their side of the partnership;
- protect the teaching-contact time available for pupils;
- prevent an unreasonable increase in teachers' workloads.

ITE Agreements

Agreements should be between HEIs and the *schools*, not with individual teachers from those schools. Where an ITE agreement is being made between a school and a HEI, the headteacher, in consultation with the governing body, should ensure that

- the written contract or statement of partnership is agreed and is subject to annual review;
- at least one term's notice is required before withdrawal;
- procedures are agreed in case there are insufficient numbers of trainees available or unforeseen circumstances, such as sickness, prevent the partnership agreement being fulfilled;

- the provision of non-staffing resources and support, such as library access and reprographic facilities, is agreed;
- the money received by the school for ITE is accounted for separately;
- 'transparency' is maximised by having the accounts held open to all staff and governors;
- the school side of the agreement can be carried out within the resources allocated, taking account of benefits and actual costs.

It will also be good practice for trainees to receive a clear statement of their entitlement during their course and details of any share of responsibilities between schools and HEIs.

MENTORS IN ITE

If a school is to be involved in ITE, it will need to appoint mentors or teacher-tutors from within the existing staff. A mentor's role depends on how the school's role in training is defined and on its ability to balance that role effectively with its central purpose of providing high-quality education for pupils. The appointment of a mentor should be subject to fair and open selection procedures. A mentor or teacher-tutor should be an experienced teacher with a sound knowledge of educational and curriculum developments, although the best mentors tend to be those with 2–3 years' teaching experience, who can remember what it was like to be a trainee and who do not have any other responsibilities.

The Role of the Mentor

Set out under four headings, below, is a summary of the guidance given to school-based mentors by the School of Education, Oxford Brookes University (1999a).

Evaluate to move forward

Without the support of a mentor, trainees can easily find themselves at a loss over how to move forward in their teaching. This tendency of performance to plateau-out can happen with any trainee teacher, irrespective of ability level, and help with evaluating their lessons is one useful contribution mentors can make. Trainee teachers have only their necessarily limited experience of class teaching on which to base judgements about successful and less-successful pedagogical strategies. If a particular approach has worked, trainees might tend to repeat it uncritically and so neglect to devise alternative and more exciting strategies. If an approach has not worked, the same tendency might lead trainees to abandon any idea of trying to improve it.

Either way, trainees can end up with only a limited range of ideas and approaches which they are confident of using. This can a negative effect both on their own teaching development and on pupils' attitude and expectations.

We all like to know how we are teaching. Even experienced teachers welcome the support and advice of their colleagues. Trainees who are given constructive feedback by a mentor who observes them teach find it easier to see how they might develop their strengths and seek alternative strategies in areas where they are experiencing difficulty.

Planning

Planning is central to all forms of teaching. Mentors can help trainees to plan more efficiently, for example by explaining how the content of their own previous lessons relates to the National Curriculum. This can be used to lead into what will be taught in the trainee's lesson, and what targets need to be set for pupils in terms of process and skills. Trainees will also require guidance on how to make the lesson effective, the best approaches to classroom organisation, management and teaching. Assessment and evaluation procedures will also need to be considered. Ideas can generally be found in mentoring handbooks issued by the partnership's HEI. Past evaluations will need to be reviewed, as also will school-based documentation from the subject co-ordinators and their evaluations of trainees. Mentors should work in close collaboration with their colleagues. Above all, mentors should encourage trainee teachers to value and build on their strengths and overcome their weaknesses.

To help trainees build effective differentiation into their planning, mentors might look at the next two or three weeks' lessons with classes and with trainees identify the key points that whole classes should cover in that period, and those points which you expect only some classes/pupils to address in detail. Then ways to build-in additional support for weaker pupils and extension material for other pupils may be devised.

Mentors might help trainees identify any teaching approaches they are inclined to avoid because they lack confidence in, for instance, the related management and organisational skills. The mentor should suggest activities and management strategies. A useful starting-point can be to focus on a small group of pupils which is to be taught by the trainee, who then observes the mentor, or a colleague, teaching a group parallel to the trainee's. This is particularly effective in helping trainees with management and organisational strategies.

It is important that mentors recognise the many apects of teaching practice with which colleagues can help, and also that not all ideas have to come direct from the mentor.

Finally (in relation to planning), mentors might

- ask questions which require trainees to analyse and reflect on their teaching, and to focus on realistic goals;
- remind trainees to watch out for things that tip the balance of a lesson one way or another, and to plan to include or avoid such things in future lessons;
- remind themselves to use the profile of competences as a checklist, but not to slavishly go through the entire document every week.

Teaching

When teaching, trainees will require that mentors

- regularly observe lessons taught by trainees, with an agreed – limited – number of factors to focus and give feedback on: indeed, in most cases a single focus is enough;
- use one column of the lesson-observation sheet to make detailed notes and the comments' section for the key points extracted;
- work with them collaboratively to share the teaching of some lessons or classes – this is especially important for trainees in their first school placement.

Further assistance can be given by sharing the lead in a lesson, so that the mentor may introduce the lesson and the trainee teacher then to lead an activity, before handing back to the mentor for the next phase. It is, however, essential to make explicit to the pupils exactly who, trainee or mentor, is in control at any point. This is a useful way of dealing with a difficult class, or of helping a trainee to observe management strategies and lesson progression.

Where necessary, splitting the group – either with both of you in the class-room or, if another space is available, in different rooms – will offer opportunities for differentiation, by task and by response.

Alternatively, trainees may learn from the circus of activities whereby pupils are split into groups, within the same room or in several rooms, to tackle a series of activities over the course of the lesson. This is a particularly effective way of giving Year 11 pupils practice in specific skills or levels of tasks. Both mentor and trainee are then free to circulate round the groups or to lead any of the activities.

Team teaching, in which both mentor and trainee share the teaching for all or part of a lesson, is also a useful approach to developing trainees' skills.

Additional mentorship can be provided by the subject mentor – the member of staff in the trainee's own subject area who, in liaison with the training manager, is mainly responsible for supporting the trainee during school placements. Usually, the subject mentor is the member of staff who has most contact with the trainee in terms of both teaching and discussion time. Where trainees work with several teachers during a school placement, the mentor is the key person with whom they can plan and evaluate their teaching.

Mentors are responsible for

- organising a teaching timetable for trainees and arranging experiences for them which will implement the programme set out in the course handbook;
- engaging trainees in discussion which will encourage them to link theory and practice;
- helping trainees develop effective self-evaluation skills;
- liaising with any other subject colleagues with whom the trainees are working;
- regular monitoring of the trainee's progress;
- completing the summative sections of assessment documents in collaboration with the trainee and training manager.

The mentoring network in a school

Figure 5.1 indicates the main contacts an effective mentor can be expected to have in a school. There is need for a network of pastoral tutors, professional tutors, mentors, trainees and college tutors so that trainees receive comprehensive support and challenge.

Mentorship, by implication, confers status: mentors therefore should be aware of themselves as exemplars of 'good practice' who have

- the ability to counsel, support and, where necessary, direct trainees, facilitate their development and evaluate their practice;
- the ability to assess formally the development of the trainee against a list of requisite professional competences;
- the maturity and confidence to respond assertively to questions and challenges from trainees;
- sufficient knowledge of the school, its staff, departments and pupils, to introduce trainees to the routines and procedures of the institution.

Headteachers should ensure that mentors receive

- the appropriate training;
- requisite reductions in teaching load without increasing the load of colleagues (though this may be difficult in practice);
- directed time to fulfil their ITE responsibilities;
- salary recognition, where appropriate;
- ongoing support, advice and evaluation.

89

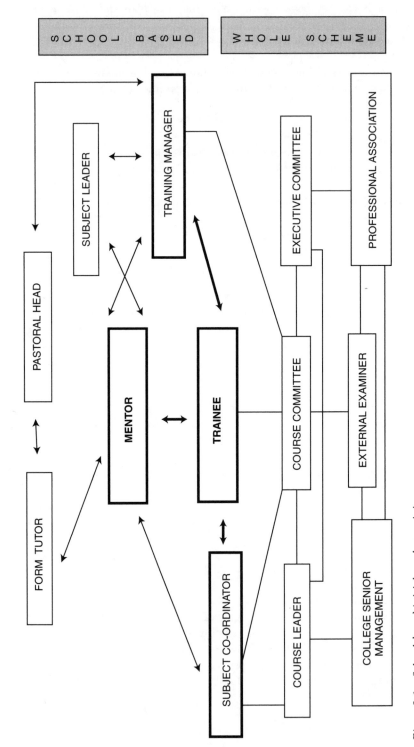

Figure 5.1 School-based initial teacher training

Source Oxford Brookes University (1998)

The number of trainees per mentor will depend on

- the mentor's other duties as a teacher;
- the prior experience of the trainees;
- the extent of the responsibilities given to the mentor within the particular partnership agreement;
- the mentor's own training and experience;
- whether or not the trainees involved are from one partnership scheme or from several;
- the amount of directed time allocated to the mentoring of trainees.

Participation in ITE can enhance schools and contribute towards professional development and overall morale. The purpose of ITE, however, is to provide an effective, supportive and stimulating start to a teacher's career.

Where the criteria outlined above cannot be met, the headteacher should not recommend a school's involvement in teacher training. Where these criteria can be met, and the tasks undertaken in a spirit of co-operation and mutual support, those involved in decision-making and action can feel a sense of ownership and can understand the direction in which the organisation is heading.

THE FUTURE

The government's Green Paper *Teachers Meeting the Challenge of Change* (DfEE 1998b), in which proposals to make ITE more flexible and more rigorous so that new teachers are equipped with the skills to teach well are outlined. The proposals include:

- new national tests for all trainee teachers to guarantee high-level skills in numeracy, literacy and information and communication technology (ICT);
- new pre-course provision for trainee teachers;
- reviewing procedures for Qualified Teacher Status;
- development of a network of schools pioneering innovative practice in school-led teacher training;
- encouraging the widest possible range of applicants through more flexible training courses;
- extending employment-based routes into teaching.

The government also intends to introduce, via the proposed Advanced Skills scheme (discussed below and detailed in Chapter 6), a new national fast-track mechanism to attract outstanding graduates into teaching and to move outstanding teachers quickly through the profession.

Recognising the Contribution of Schools

The government recognises that most schools contribute to ITT, whether as partner schools with HEIs, providers of school-centred training or of training for entrants on employment-based routes. It intends to review funding arrangements to ensure that it recognise the role of schools as equal partners. In particular, it will consult on the case for the direct funding of HEI–school partnerships rather than channelling the funding for partner schools through the HEIs.

The government wants to encourage good and innovative practice in school-led ITT. The government plans to establish a network of high-quality training schools, with additional investment in ICT, to provide mentor training, direct on-line advice to trainees and the dissemination of best practice to satellite schools and to HEIs. These schools would also develop a research function, developing good practice on induction and in-service training.

Extending Flexibility

The government intends (DfEE 1998b) that training routes will be diverse and flexible so that training can be matched to the needs and circumstances of all those with the potential to succeed as teachers. Alongside the existing one-year Certificate the government proposes to develop, and make available from 2000, new modular courses for postgraduate teacher training which are structured in shorter segments and have flexible start and end points.

When the new modules are available, the government will ask HEIs to look at ways of integrating teacher-training modules into their undergraduate degrees so that students can gain experience and recognition by working as paid associates in schools while taking the relevant modules of the teaching course. An undergraduate studying mathematics, for example, could opt to take some teacher-training modules during his or her degree course, and so gain accreditation towards a postgraduate teaching qualification.

In addition, the government will encourage both graduates and under-graduates to act as paid part-time teaching associates. This would give serving teachers a pool of adult support workers through whom at the same time they would have access to the latest developments in particular subject areas or to particular expertise – for example, in the creative arts. The government believes that this will provide valuable experience for schools and students alike and also enable students to find out for themselves whether teaching is the career for them. The government intends, from next year, to pilot the use of students as teaching assistants in Education Action Zones.

The government is determined that employment-based routes into teaching should be recognised as providing high-quality preparation for entry into the profession, open to those who may not be able to pursue a more traditional teacher training course.

A National Fast Track

The government considers (DfEE 1998b) that teaching is a career which should attract a greater share of the most talented graduates and offer rapid advancement to teachers of exceptional ability. The government proposes, therefore, to create a new fast-track which will offer extra training and support to the most promising trainees to enable them to reach the performance threshold more rapidly. In return, fast-track entrants would be asked to accept supplementary contracts with a longer working year and greater mobility. The fast track would be open both to recruits to ITE and to excellent serving teachers below the threshold. The government envisages two ways of entering the scheme:

- through a national graduate recruitment programme;
- through applications by, or nominations of, those showing exceptional talent in teacher training or in their early years as teachers.

The fast-track will link to the Advanced Skills Teacher programme introduced to schools in 1998–99. The government will need to evaluate the effectiveness of both initiatives in the context of lifelong learning and the raising of standards of achievement in schools. The response from the teaching unions to these proposals has, however, been negative, particularly because both are linked to performance-related pay.

SUMMARY

This chapter has described the first stage in a teacher's career. Qualified Teacher Status is a requirement for all those who teach in a maintained school, and as such represents the first national professional qualification in the government's framework of standards and qualifications for teachers.

In December 1998, the government published its Green Paper *Teachers Meeting the Challenge of Change* (DfEE 1998b) in which it proposed to make ITT more flexible and more rigorous so that all new teachers acquire the skills required to teach well. The government considers that teaching is a career that should attract a greater share of the most talented graduates and offer rapid advancement to teachers of exceptional ability. The government proposes, therefore, to create a new fast-track which will offer extra training and support to the most promising and so enable them to reach the performance threshold more rapidly. The fast-track is linked to the Advanced Skills Teacher programme introduced to schools in 1998–99 (see Chapter 6).

Chapter 6 provides guidance for practitioners in determining their approach to professional development. The introduction of a Learning Account as suggested by the government (DfEE 1998b) emphasises how important it is for teachers to know and understand what is available and likely to prove effective.

6

PRACTITIONERS

INTRODUCTION

This chapter focuses on the role of the practitioner within a learning organisation and considers the position of practitioners in relation to professional development. The chapter summarises the diverse range of professional development opportunities available to practitioners, including: the Career Entry Profile; induction; the Advanced Skills Teacher programme; professional competence assessments; award-bearing courses; and research. Such opportunities for career development will contribute to a learning organisation only if managed effectively (see Chapter 1) and if all practitioners are required to take responsibility for their own development. The government supports this principle and plans to introduce Learning Accounts for all teachers that will fund their professional development and training. Quality management will be necessary to provide opportunities for practitioners to contribute, through professional development, to the effectiveness of their schools.

THE CAREER ENTRY PROFILE

The key role of the Career Entry Profile (CEP) is to plan a new teacher's professional development. From September 1999 CEPs are to be used in the context of the new statutory induction arrangements for NQTs.

All providers of ITT will award to newly qualified teachers (NQTs) a Teacher Training Agency CEP when they successfully complete their initial training. Only those trainees who gain Qualified Teacher Status (QTS) receive a CEP, the purpose of which is to support the transition from initial training to teaching and continuing professional development. The CEP will afford such support by

- providing information, in relation to the standards for the award of QTS, about new teachers' strengths and their priorities for further professional development;
- requiring new teachers to set their objectives for professional development and prepare an action plan for induction.

The government (TTA 1999b) does not anticipate any major changes to the documentation and the existing structure is likely to remain. Perhaps most importantly, the purpose of the CEP is the same: to support schools and NQTs, working together, to:

- make the best use of the skills and abilities NQTs bring with them;
- build on a new teacher's achievements in relation to the standards for the award of QTS and, from September 1999, the standards for induction;
- recognise the importance of effective professional development from the earliest possible stage in a NQT's career, and consider the new teacher's longer term professional development;
- devise a focused and individualised programme of development, which will improve the NQT's practice in areas identified for development during the first year of teaching;
- make sustained and significant progress in the quality of a new teacher's performance in relation to the teacher's own targets, the school's development plan, and local and national priorities.

The TTA's Career Entry Profile is not intended to replace the references for NQTs which ITE providers give to prospective employers. Under the statutory induction arrangements:

- The headteacher will be responsible for ensuring that a programme of monitoring, support and assessment is in place which takes account of a NQT's Career Entry Profile.
- The induction tutor will be responsible for supporting the NQT and helping to implement a programme of monitoring, support and review based on the action plan set out in the CEP.
- The NQT will be expected to make the CEP available to the school and to work with the induction tutor in using the profile to set objectives for the induction period. NQTs should make an active contribution to, and be fully engaged in, their professional development during the induction period.

The information contained in the CEP is presented in three sections.

Section A (completed by the ITE provider and the NQT) gives a summary of the NQT's initial teacher training, including any distinctive features of that training.

Section B (agreed between the ITT provider and the NQT) summarises the NQT's strengths and priorities for further professional development.

Section C (agreed between the school and the NQT) consists of an action plan, including objectives, for the induction period.

Following completion of ITT and the award of Qualified Teacher Status NQTs enter their period of induction.

INDUCTION

From September 1999 teachers achieving QTS will be required to complete a statutory induction year, during which time the inductee will teach a timetable which is 90 per cent of the normal teaching load, and will have targeted training and support based on the needs identified in the CEP. Following a series of formal reviews, the head will make a recommendation to the appropriate body reflecting professional opinion about the degree to which an inductee has met the induction standards. Successful teachers will, from the following year, be appraised under the new appraisal system. The final induction review will be used to set objectives which, in turn, become the basis for future appraisal. Further regulations and guidance will be issued by the government.

Induction is not a new initiative. The National Union of Teachers issued a framework for good practice by schools and LEAs in relation to induction (NUT 1993b), summarised here as follows: Schools and LEAs should avoid placing NQTs in supply or peripatetic posts; also unsuitable for NQTs without special support are posts which present unusual problems of discipline or require special teaching techniques. Schools should establish guidance and training for those involved in interviewing and appointing new teachers and for those assuming responsibilities as professional tutors or mentors. Schools should also ensure that NQTs demonstrate their proficiency in teaching classes of a size normal for the school and that are closely related to the age-group and subject for which they have been trained. It is important that schools and LEAs set up induction programmes which make differentiated provision, based on an analysis of individual need, to support new teachers from widely diverse backgrounds and experience; schools and LEAs should determine their respective responsibilities for the induction training each is expected to provide, and its timing. Finally, monitoring and evaluation procedures are required to identify good practice and make possible its dissemination.

Furthermore, schools and LEAs should pay particular attention to the impact of the local management of schools (LMS) on their relationship, so that there are no gaps in their responsibilities for the appointment and induction of teachers. This can be achieved through monitoring and reporting procedures which ensure that LEAs are aware of and able to adequately support all NQTs in schools maintained by them. Following induction, managers should agree on the professional skills that are to be acquired by NQTs by the end of their first year of teaching to help each plan their support. Teacher-training institutions can help by clearly identifying the skills possessed by their students who have just been awarded QTS. Managers should also look carefully at the provision of training for NQTs to ensure that it is efficiently and effectively provided.

More specifically, the school should make available to an appointed NQT

- the time to visit the school to meet the headteacher, the head of department, where appropriate, and fellow members of staff;
- information from the school, in the form of a staff handbook or similar document, relevant to the school's curriculum organisation and management, the staff structure, the staff training and development policy, discipline, extra-curricular activities, relationships with the local community;
- adequate notice of the timetable to be taught;
- all curricular documents, including statutory documents relating to the National Curriculum, relevant to the subjects he or she will teach;
- information about equipment and other resources available for use, including information technology;
- information about support and supervision provided by the school and, in the case of LEA-maintained schools, any additional support provided by the LEA.

Ideally, induction should be viewed as a whole-school responsibility. It is important that school policies and joint aims and objectives be discussed at the earliest opportunity with the NQT, and written policies agreed on a whole-school basis, e.g. for curricular areas, should be made available. Of particular importance is the need to agree on

- who will be the teacher-tutor; what will be her or his formal responsibilities in relation to the new teacher and, if the teacher-tutor is distinct from the mentor, who will adopt the latter's less formal 'professional friend' role;
- what training this person requires;
- the procedures for observing and evaluating the progress of the new teacher (these should be made clear to the NQT at the outset);
- the balance between written 'evidence' of progress and casual observation which will be required;
- the procedures to be followed where difficulties are identified.

Figure 6.1 illustrates the sources of support available for NQTs in the process of induction. These include school and LEA induction programmes, as defined above, and mentoring and team development (discussed further in Chapter 11).

Inspectors and advisers in many LEAs have considerable experience of successful induction schemes for new teachers. Their expertise and experience should underpin the future development of induction programmes for NQTs.

The government expects most teachers, following induction, to progress up the salary scale in annual steps. Maintaining this rate of progress will depend on a teacher's demonstration of sustained satisfactory performance in annual appraisals. The government proposes that this opportunity will be open to all teachers performing to a very high standard, not just to those on the new fast-track. In cases where elements of a teacher's performance are demonstrated by the appraisal process to be unsatisfactory, or where competency proceedings have started, the salary increment should be withheld.

THE ADVANCED SKILLS TEACHER SCHEME

The Advanced Skills Teacher (AST) grade was created by the DfEE in 1998 to provide a career path for excellent teachers wanting to remain classroom

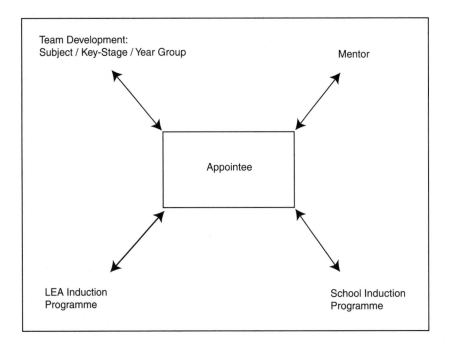

Figure 6.1   Areas of support for newly appointed staff

practitioners who pass a rigorous assessment against national standards. In the context of a learning organisation, this provides practitioners with the opportunity to develop their career without moving into management. Such opportunities are to be welcomed as major contributions to the creation of a learning community, and this particular scheme may be considered a means of retaining and developing good staff. The skills of these more experienced and able practitioners may, in addition, be deployed to assist those in need of further guidance and development.

Advanced Skills Teachers will be classroom practitioners with extra duties, such as acting as mentors for NQTs and advising other teachers, but no management duties. They could spend up to 20 per cent of their time in schools other than their own to help disseminate best practice. Teachers will be able to apply for AST posts only after they have been licensed following an assessment process. The government intends that only a small number of teachers will become ASTs. The AST grade is now being introduced in specialist schools and in Education Action Zones: 100 ASTs are expected to be in post by the end of 1999, with an expansion to 5,000 by the year 2000 and a total of 10,000 in the longer term.

The government has stated that each AST is formally required to perform an outreach function and to spread good practice (DfEE 1999). How this is to be achieved is not prescribed centrally. Some valuable examples of innovative approaches have already been identified during the introductory phase. The government reports (ibid.) that ASTs are already

- developing and delivering in-service training;
- demonstrating good classroom practice, both in person and through ICT links to other schools and teacher training institutions;
- designing and testing new teaching materials.

Governing bodies have discretion over how many leadership positions to create in line with their own staffing structures and budgets. Similarly the government expects ASTs to be included as leaders of teaching and learning. At primary level, the leadership group may well not exceed the headteacher and any deputy or AST, though the larger schools may co-opt the heads of infant and junior departments, too.

A single pay spine may cover all leadership posts including ASTs, with the top points available only to headteachers. Governing bodies would decide a suitable pay range for each post on the basis of national guidance and advice from the headteacher. Pay progression for all staff, including ASTs, will be based on annual performance reviews against individual targets, including those relating to pupil performance, and the outcomes of the annual appraisal process. Given the prospect of higher pay, it is expected that ASTs will

- give masterclasses out of school hours;
- help other teachers develop teaching styles with high expectations;
- improve continuity and progression between the primary and secondary phases.

ASTs are to be a valuable resource for schools in need of excellent teachers to help turn them round, but which have experienced problems recruiting staff of the right calibre.

Practice

The AST scheme is to be funded by the government for two years. For each AST post the school will receive £6,000 a year to cover increased pay (not all of this necessarily goes to the 'superteachers' themselves) and a further £6,000 to provide staff cover so that an AST can spend one day a week either helping colleagues or visiting other schools.

To date, all ASTs have been internal appointments. Some schools in Education Action Zones are interested in offering AST grades to external candidates, though this introduces the complication that they have first to be appointed to a school post and then go through a separate process before receiving the AST grade.

The assessment process for 'superteachers' is designed to avoid any charges of cronyism. Headteachers will not be able to award AST status to their favourites, as all appointments have to be approved by Westminster Education, the independent consultants appointed by the government. Thus far, two teachers proposed by their schools have not met the requirements.

Assessment will be made against national standards characterising experienced and high-performing classroom teachers. The standards are intended to apply in all maintained schools, including special schools, and to part-time as well as to full-time staff.

Candidates will be expected to show excellence across several criteria: teaching ability, pupils' results, subject knowledge, planning, maintaining discipline, assessment, and advising and supporting colleagues. Assessors observe lessons taught by candidates and talk to other staff at the school. In an unusual departure from the normal practice for appointments, the assessor will also consult parents and pupils. Some might imagine that pupils would be tempted to recommend only those teachers who give them an easy time. Time will tell how effective this initiative can be in creating learning organisations.

The Performance Threshold

An important initiative in the professional development of teachers is the introduction of a performance threshold. The government proposes (DfEE 1999) that teachers who, for at least one year, have held nine incremental points for qualifications and experience will be eligible to apply to cross the performance threshold. Successful candidates will need to show a high degree of competence, achievement and commitment resulting in positive pupil outcomes. The government believes that achieving the threshold standards will be sufficiently demanding that more than one attempt is likely to be required. The government expects that in time the majority of teachers will meet the standards and pass the threshold.

Teachers who achieve the threshold standards are expected to be highly effective classroom practitioners and to command a wide authority with pupils across the school. They will have an established track record of good results and will have made a significant contribution, through their teaching, to their schools' targets, policies, ethos and aims. They will be up to date with both academic and pedagogic developments in their subjects and specialisms. They will have a wide repertoire of teaching techniques and use relevant evidence and data to improve their teaching in order to raise the standards of pupils' achievements. They will also demonstrate professional understanding of the effects of their teaching and assessment approaches, and be proactive in working with others, inside and outside of the school, to secure their pupils' progress.

Threshold assessment will be a comprehensive exercise which is recognised as distinct from other professional development initiatives. An application by a teacher seeking to demonstrate that he or she has met all the criteria set out in the threshold standards will be supported by a portfolio of information about that teacher's performance, including classroom observation, analysis of pupils' results over time, and indicators of the teacher's commitment to professional development and its impact on classroom performance. The government anticipates that in time all of this information will be available through the new appraisal system.

The government proposes (DfEE 1999) the following stages for threshold assessment:

1   The teacher applies to be assessed and prepares a portfolio of evidence demonstrating achievement against the national standards.
2   The teacher's senior manager (where this person is not the headteacher) offers an assessment of the candidate.
3   The headteacher decides whether the applicant meets the threshold standards.
4   A qualified assessor considers the school's overall operation of performance management and at the individual's application decides whether or not to confirm the headteacher's judgement. The final decision rests with the assessor.

Threshold assessment will therefore be conducted by the head of the school, subject to review by a trained and qualified external assessor. The head will judge whether the teacher meets all the threshold standards. This will be done on the basis of the evidence in the teacher's application, including available appraisal statements, the head's own knowledge of that teacher's performance and written advice from the teacher's senior manager.

The head will prepare a written recommendation for each candidate in relation to the national standards, giving the reasons underlying the judgement and referring to the relevant evidence. These recommendations are to remain confidential and at this stage should not be communicated to the candidates. Heads may want to review borderline candidates in detail with the external assessor. In large schools the head may want to ask appropriate members of the senior management team to help with the initial work, but the judgement in each case will remain the headteacher's personal responsibility. Once the head has made recommendations on the school's applicants, the external assessor will review

- the school's overall performance management;
- the school's procedures for threshold assessments;
- the portfolio evidence of each applicant.

The assessor will also decide on the basis of several factors whether a more detailed review, including lesson observations and interviews with applicants, is needed to reach a secure judgement on each candidate's performance against the threshold standards.

PROFESSIONAL COMPETENCE

The assessment of a teacher's ability to teach is not new: the competence movement introduced to this country by the National Educational Assessment Centre has been considering this issue since the mid-1980s. The principle of professional competence as a means of assessment implies that teachers' career and professional development may be determined according to their professional skills and abilities. This is a particular approach to the assessment of professional development needs. Teaching competences are defined by Hayes in Cave and Wilkinson (1991) as 'a generic knowledge, trait, self-image, social role or skill of a person that is causally linked to superior performance on the job'. A definition more closely related to work is given by the Teacher Training Agency (1994):

> competence is a description of something which a person who works in a given occupational area should be able to do. It is a description of an action, behaviour or outcome through which the person should

be able to demonstrate the ability to perform work activities to the standards required in employment.

Figure 6.2 indicates the professional competences of a successful teacher. A professional development policy based on competence would use this as a framework for assessing and determining a practitioner's developmental needs. For example, were it to be agreed by and his or her manager that a teacher had a weakness in classroom management and was therefore in need of developing this professional competence, training would be given to meet this need. Assessing current competences may be considered an effective means of developing teachers and managers.

Practitioners may also consider their own management development needs on the basis of competence. The National Educational Assessment Centre developed an assessment of competence as a diagnostic tool for aspiring middle management in education. The process was adapted from a model which has been used for more than twenty years in America by the National Association of Secondary School Principals (NASSP). It may be summarised as follows:

Professional competences of the successful teacher:

Knowledge and understanding:

1	Knowledge of children and their learning
2	Subject knowledge
3	Knowledge of the curriculum
4	Knowledge of the teacher's role

Skills:
1	Subject application
2	Classroom methodology
3	Class management
4	Assessment and recording

Figure 6.2   Professional competences of the effective teacher

1 *Administrative competences*

- Problem analysis: the ability to seek out and analyse relevant data to determine the important elements of a situation.

- Judgement: the ability to reach logical conclusions from the information available and make high-quality decisions; to set priorities; to show caution where necessary.
- Organisational ability and decisiveness: the ability to plan and schedule effectively; to delegate appropriately; to recognise when a decision is required and to act upon it.

2 *Interpersonal competences*
- Leadership: the ability to motivate others and involve them in the accomplishment of tasks by securing the general acceptance of ideas. Leadership also requires a disposition to engage in proactive behaviour.
- Sensitivity: an ability to perceive needs, concerns and problems from differing viewpoints and to act accordingly; to value the contribution of others.

3 *Communicative competences*
- Oral communication: the ability to make clear oral presentations of facts or ideas.
- Written communication: the ability to express ideas clearly and appropriately for different audiences in writing.

In addition, the NEAC diagnostic tool recommends that such individual dispositions as personal breadth and level of stress tolerance are reported. Motivation and educational values also should be commented on but not recorded.

All of the activities used in this assessment process are work-related: discussion groups, in-tray exercises, presentations and written responses to a series of questions. The report thus generated presents a competence profile. The conclusion offers points for consideration in devising an action plan for development, and encourages participants to tackle recommendations in a structured way.

AWARD BEARING COURSES: TEACHERS AS RESEARCHERS

As indicated in the Green Paper (DfEE 1998b), when planning staff development for teachers and support staff award-bearing courses and research opportunities should be considered. The difficulty for teachers and support staff is how to use their experience to gain awards and develop research opportunities. While it is a mistake to equate either learning or achievement with qualifications alone, teachers and support staff need to reflect on the learning that takes place in the classroom. Time will have to be invested in providing opportunities for staff to reflect on their practice and to utilise such experiences in the context of awards and research opportunities (Blandford 1998b).

The government report on Lifelong Learning (NAGCELL 1997) states: 'an unnecessary barrier to awards and research is created by the number of qualifications and the language of research'. A learning culture should be accessible to all members of the school community; this would enable staff to develop knowledge, understanding, skills, and abilities related to research on teaching and learning. A learning culture should not be confined to particular places, methods or forms of learning. Schools should see themselves as an important part of the wider network of partners in education. Mechanisms should be identified to assist staff in schools in developing the skills to promote research opportunities.

HEIs have a particular contribution to make in extending knowledge and skills through excellence in teaching, research and dissemination. Commitment to strengthening the quality of the teaching profession and to continuing professional development is essential. In this context award-bearing courses have many advantages: for example, they provide

- a sharp and intensive stimulus to learning;
- opportunities for developing skills or understanding that are not available on-the-job;
- flexibility of design for intensive learning;
- contexts for the spin-off of learning with and by professional people other than workplace colleagues;
- an alternative to learning on-the-job.

The number and range of award-bearing courses in education is, however, potentially confusing. HEIs are in competition to fill the places on their courses and to have a research record that is rated by the academic community. Figure 6.3 illustrates HEIs' awards in relation to the national standards and qualifications and the National Vocational Qualification (NVQ). Developed from a model presented in the Dearing Review (National Committee of Inquiry into Higher Education 1997), this is an incremental approach to professional development.

It can be seen that there is significant overlap between awards, so that a possible way forward is to look for multiple outcomes, i.e. using the same or similar material and experiences for more than one award. As an example, the TTA has agreed to allow NPQH candidates to submit Master's-level dissertations and assignments, where applicable, in part fulfilment for the award. This is an excellent use of a teacher's expertise, leading to both academic and professional qualifications.

Teacher Training Agency national standards	Type of programme	Level	Award-bearing courses	NVQ Level
LPSH	Taught or by Research	H8	Doctorate	5
HEADLAMP	Taught or by Research	H7	MPhil	5
NPQH	Taught or by Research	H6	Master's degree	5
NPQSL / NPQSENCO	S, P, C or Conversion	H5	Postgraduate / Diploma	4–5
AST	S, P, C or Conversion	H4	Postgraduate / Higher Honours	4
NQT	S, P, or C	H3	Honours degree	4
	S, P, C or B	H2	Bachelor's degree	4
	S, P, C or B	H1	Certificate	3–4
	S, P, C or B		City and Guilds	2

Figure 6.3 Award-bearing courses, national standards and NVQs

Key: S = Single subject P = Subject leading to professional status C = Combined subjects
B = Broad range of subjects

Masters and Doctorates in Education

Phillips and Pugh (1988) summarise the significance of the degree levels available in a British University: a BA, BSc or BEd degree shows that the recipient has obtained a *general* education; the MA or MSc degree is a license to practise; and a PhD is a licence to teach in a university. The majority of HEIs in England and Wales that provide teacher education within their schools of education offer M-level courses for practising teachers to develop their knowledge and understanding of education theory and research, and thus to inform practice. Some courses may focus on education management, while others focus on specialist subject areas. Teachers can study at a university or opt for distance-learning packages.

Having successfully completed a course at M-level, teachers can extend their academic education to doctorate level. There are currently two distinct approaches to doctorates for educationalists: the traditional PhD (Doctor of Philosophy) and the EdD (Doctor of Education). The former requires independent study towards the completion of a thesis which makes an original contribution to the field studied. The EdD is a taught modular course offered to senior education professionals by approximately eighteen universities.

Award-bearing courses will provide practitioners with an opportunity to develop and enhance their knowledge, understanding, skills and abilities. These developments will also assist the school in raising standards. Thesis and dissertations can (and should) focus on practitioner issues, and therefore impact on schools as learning organisations.

Teachers are busy professionals. Working full-time and studying part-time can be very difficult. Practitioner researchers will require the full support of family and friends; they may require also financial support from their institution, their LEA or their school through the Standards Fund. Educational study and research should relate to practice and the needs of the school as identified in the SDP. Courses offer participants the opportunity to be challenged, stretched and excited in a college environment.

Before embarking on a course, it is important to gather as much information as possible, for example by visiting universities and talking to potential course leaders and supervisors. It is also useful to read dissertations and theses in one's area of interest to determine what will be required for the award. The work required of the individual at post-graduate levels is considerable and demanding, and upheavals such as those incurred in changing jobs or moving house should not be planned to coincide with a course.

Academic study should relate to practice; practitioner researchers should be clear about their aims and what they will do with the qualification. Think 'What next?'.

RESEARCH

Teachers are active participants in school life at every level and so are in a position to influence and engage in educational research. Researchers in education receive £35m per annum from the combined coffers of the Higher Education Funding Council for England, the Economic and Social Research Council (ESRC), the Department for Education and Employment, the National Foundation for Educational Research and the TTA. Yet Hargreaves (1996) believes that teaching is not a research-based profession. The TTA is attempting to address this issue through Teacher Research Grants.

Teacher Research Grants

According to Millett (1996b), the TTA has identified the following objectives:

- to increase the amount of classroom-based research relevant to improving the quality of teaching and learning;

- to raise awareness of what high-quality research can contribute to teaching;
- to make research findings more accessible to teachers;
- to develop teachers' skills in conducting, interpreting and using research designed to foster improved classroom practice.

The TTA is committed to developing teaching as a profession which is guided by systematic evidence and effective classroom research (Cordingley 1999). This requires

- increased research in areas relevant to improving the quality of teaching and learning;
- raising awareness of what high-quality research can contribute to teaching;
- making research findings more accessible to teachers;
- developing teachers' skills in conducting, interpreting and using research, designed to foster improved classroom practice.

The TTA's Teacher Research Grants provides up to thirty grants a year to enable teachers to undertake small-scale classroom-based research projects and to ensure that their findings are made accessible to colleagues. The purpose of the scheme is to increase the stock of high-quality small-scale classroom research carried out by teachers, to raise other teachers' interest in such work and to extend the debate about the role of teachers in classroom research.

Awards reflect the TTA's emphasis on improving pedagogic practice. The TTA encourages teachers to develop projects which concentrate on specific aspects of effective teaching practice in relation to how pupils learn. Projects should be directly aimed at improving pedagogy and practice in the class-room.

SUMMARY

This chapter has considered the position of practitioners in the context of the national standards for teachers and the development opportunities offered by HEIs. Such opportunities for career development will contribute to a learning organisation only if managed effectively (see Chapter 1), requiring all practitioners to take responsibility for their own development.

The AST grade was created by the DfEE in 1998 to provide a career path for excellent teachers wishing to continue as classroom practitioners and who pass a rigorous assessment against national standards. In the context of a learning organisation this provides practitioners with the opportunity to develop their career without moving into management.

As indicated in the Green Paper (DfEE 1998b), when planning staff development for teachers and support staff, award-bearing courses and research opportunities should be considered. Teachers are active participants in school life at every level and are in a position to influence and engage in educational research.

Further, management training leading to national qualifications provided by TTA regional centres provides a framework for the career development of teachers who aspire to become headteachers. Evaluations of these schemes are presented in Chapter 7.

7

LEADERSHIP

INTRODUCTION

The development of national standards for headteachers began in 1995 with the introduction of a training programme called the Headteacher Leadership and Management Programme (HEADLAMP) for those recently appointed to headships. The government, as part of its drive to improve schools, has since introduced the National Professional Qualification for Headship (NPQH) and the Leadership Programme for Serving Headteachers (LPSH). This chapter provides an examination of each of these three qualifications, based on the government's evaluation procedures and research. The examination of the leadership schemes within the national standards for teachers should provide further guidance to practitioners on training and induction opportunities leading to, and beyond headship. This chapter will consider the effectiveness of the schemes, which may assist practitioners, managers and governors when directing staff towards such programmes. Crucially, all issues raised in this chapter relate directly to TQM and the management of a learning organisation. The chapter begins with a brief account of the background to current training initiatives for school leaders.

BACKGROUND

The first attempts, during the 1980s, to provide support for headteachers – beyond the initiatives of individual LEAs – were led by the National Development Centre for Education Management and Policy (NDCEMP). However, by the end of that decade, only 11 per cent of the target population had participated in such development opportunities (Criessen and Ellison 1996; Male 1997).

In 1990 the government began an investigation of alternative approaches. The School Management Task Force (SMTF) undertook a national audit of school leaders. At the end of its two-year investigation, the SMTF was commissioned to oversee the Headteacher Mentoring Scheme, a new initiative designed to assist newly appointed headteachers through the provision of a trained mentor in the form of an experienced headteacher (Male 1997). Despite many valuable lessons (see Bolam et al. 1999), this scheme folded due to a lack of funding after just one year.

Induction and management development opportunities for newly appointed headteachers continued to be offered largely at the discretion of LEAs. Research into LEA management development provision for headteachers identified great diversity (see Baker 1996): in some areas there was a tradition of intensive programmes; in others, little formal activity.

The TTA, created by central government in 1994 to oversee all aspects of teacher education, developed a framework for the professional development of teachers. This included standards for aspiring, newly qualified and serving headteachers. The TTA considered that all headteachers, even the best, would benefit from further targeted training and development. The TTA developed a threefold national strategy, underpinned by the national standards for headteachers, intended for

1   aspiring headteachers (National Professional Qualification for Headship) – the initial training phase;
2   newly appointed headteachers (Headteacher Leadership and Management Programme) – the induction phase;
3   serving headteachers (Leadership Programme for Serving Headteachers) – the in-service phase.

The planned route through the framework established for headteachers is one of preparation, induction, reflection and development. The White Paper *Excellence in Schools* (DfEE 1997a) and the Green Paper (DfEE 1998b) gave the first indications of the government's intention that all prospective headteachers will undertake formal preparation and induction. The status of the TTA programmes and qualifications is currently within the legislative process, and the government intention is that the NPQH will be mandatory for headteachers by 2002.

The national standards set out the knowledge, understanding, skills and abilities which relate to key tasks of headship in five key areas (see Chapter 4). The standards are designed to serve as the focal points for the training and development of aspiring, newly appointed and serving headteachers.

The National Professional Qualification for Headship (NPQH)

The TTA introduced the NPQH in 1996, and trials took place in 1996–97. The *Report on the Outcomes of the NPQH Trials* (TTA 1998b) evaluated the programme's effectiveness as perceived by the trials' candidates and their headteachers, though as yet there has been no similar evaluation of the impact on management practices in schools of the NPQH. What follows is a summary of the findings reported (ibid.) on the trials.

The TTA found that the great majority of the trials' candidates reported positively on their experiences of the NPQH. Participants indicated clear improvements in their professional knowledge and understanding and, as a result, enhanced leadership skills and attributes, as required in the national standards. Trials' candidates reported notable beneficial impacts on their schools, including improved monitoring and evaluation procedures, a more strategic approach to development planning, improved staff development provision and a greater understanding of the requirements for headship.

Candidates overwhelmingly approved of the training where it was practical and professional. Some candidates expressed reservation in respect of areas for which the training was felt to be overly academic and theoretical. Most candidates found the needs' assessment exercise particularly rewarding, the most helpful element being the personal interview. It was felt, however, that the process would benefit from greater consistency and reliability between assessors.

Some candidates reported to the TTA that they would have appreciated fuller guidance and help in formulating the action plans resulting from their needs assessment. Training and development centres, it was thought, need to take better account of action planning during training in order to cater for candidates' individual needs. Most trials' candidates considered the training they received to be extremely effective in preparing them to meet the national standards for headteachers. However, a significant minority considered the organisation of training insufficiently matched to ongoing individual needs and phase interests (whether primary or secondary). TTA findings suggested that candidates would have welcomed an increase in feedback and formative assessment.

The support of candidates' headteachers was considered to be crucial to the development of the next generation of school leaders. Some candidates had enjoyed the full support of their headteachers, while others would have welcomed more but were loath to ask their busy headteachers. No trials' candidate reported opposition from his or her headteacher. Candidates reported their need of support, and not just from their headteachers, for the duration of the programme: those regions which had assigned mentors to candidates were particularly praised.

The TTA's evaluation established that candidates identified as the best trainers were those who set clear objectives, were well prepared, matched objectives with activities effectively and integrated relevant research and inspection findings with practice. The contributions of effective practising headteachers to the training were particularly valued. Some of the trainers used in the trials were reported to lack skills and expertise in the training of adults. The great majority of candidates managed the work required by the NPQH trials as well as performing their responsibilities in school. Some candidates commented on a negative effect experienced when there was a lack of fit between their trials' assessment tasks and school activities.

Following the evaluation process the TTA identified (1998b) the key areas and the changes required before full implementation of the qualification:

- greater consistency of practice in training and assessment within and between NPQH centres;
- streamlining of procedures and associated materials to be as straightforward and unbureaucratic as possible;
- stricter requirements of training providers to make full use of the findings of the needs assessment process and full guidance on action planning;
- action to ensure that NPQH candidates have the necessary support to undertake the qualification successfully.

Further evaluations are now required to determine the effectiveness of the programme by assessing its impact on candidates and school practices *during* and *after* the course.

HEADTEACHER LEADERSHIP AND MANAGEMENT PROGRAMME (HEADLAMP)

A study, completed by Blandford and Squire (1997), on the provision and management of HEADLAMP's funded induction and training programmes for headteacher initial appointments, from September 1995 to September 1996, and the perceptions of the participating headteachers is summarised in what follows.

The provision of induction support and management development opportunities for new headteachers was widespread in LEAs before the introduction of HEADLAMP. The study found that this remains largely unchanged, as HEADLAMP provision is being made by LEAs, HEIs and, in some areas, those diocesan boards with a tradition of providing induction and management development opportunities. The many smaller consultancies and providers registered with the TTA did not feature strongly in responses from the study sample.

The study found that LEAs had welcomed HEADLAMP, quickly developing and adapting provision to meet its requirements. Many LEAs had registered as HEADLAMP providers, and had modified or developed existing provision in order to meet TTA requirements. As a consequence of HEADLAMP funding, some LEAs were able to extend the range of induction and development opportunities offered and were able also to include headteachers other than the newly appointed in this provision. In practice, a high value was placed on the role of mentors both by LEAs and new head-teachers.

Headteacher Evaluations of HEADLAMP

Overall, the response was positive and HEADLAMP was considered to be an excellent opportunity for headteachers. The study found that the training was of value to the school as well as to the head, and participants had valued the opportunity provided by HEADLAMP to 'focus on big issues' and to develop strategies. HEADLAMP had also made it possible for respondents to access training related to their individual needs. The majority of the study sample had felt that their chosen HEADLAMP induction and course providers offered value for money.

Management of HEADLAMP

The dominant issue emerging from the study related to the management of HEADLAMP. The majority of headteachers saw themselves as managing their own HEADLAMP training, with LEAs managing the induction element. Participants valued the support in the management of the programme given by experienced headteachers, who also provided mentoring.

In practice, the study sample found the management of HEADLAMP problematic and time-consuming. The volume of administrative paperwork required by HEADLAMP was considered to be 'overwhelming' and a barrier to participation in the programme. The majority of the sample felt that the TTA could make itself more accessible to participants during the programme. Headteachers also reported an apparent lack of understanding on the part of LEAs as to what constituted HEADLAMP provision, and that LEA provision tended, as a result, to be reactive rather than proactive.

The timing of HEADLAMP caused management problems. The study concluded that the programme should be scheduled so that all participants had acclimatised to the realities of their new position following induction. A frequent comment was that new headteachers need to spend as much time as possible in school. Headteachers also believed that it is essential to know the needs of the school as a whole before selecting a development programme. Suggestions for scheduling the start of HEADLAMP ranged from one term to two years into an appointment. A three-year 'sell-by' date was a popular idea.

Conclusions of the Study

The study found that respondents valued the opportunity to participate in HEADLAMP. All recognised the importance of professional development in relation to school leadership. The range and quality of opportunities accessed by the respondents were varied, from needs analysis by professional organisations, HEI and LEAs to induction and management courses. LEAs were recognised as the most accessible providers of all three elements. Of the respondents who had experienced a greater diversity of provision, mentors, LEAs, HEIs and professional associations were cited as sources of relevant and valuable guidance and training. Only one headteacher suggested that HEI accreditation would be an advantage. Respondents found the HEAD-LAMP experience to have been positive and acknowledged the programme's contribution to the developmental needs of both the individual and his or her school.

The study has also shown that the principles of the Headteacher Leadership and Management Programme are appreciated by practitioners and advisers. The essential difficulty has been in the management of the process. The programme provides welcome funding to enable headteachers to access a range of needs analysis, induction and training opportunities. However, the dominance of LEAs and the limited awareness and contribution of governors in the planning of individual programmes have led to the pursuit of quite narrow options. There is also concern that not all LEAs have advisers with knowledge and understanding of current professional development issues.

Repeatedly the major problem was said to be HEADLAMP's two year time-scale. New heads require more time to consider and plan the training that will relate their own skill needs to the circumstances of their schools. The needs of a new head look vastly different towards the end of the first year in post. Heads may need up to two terms before they can engage in the sort of needs' analysis that provides sufficient information for a consultant to recommend the appropriate programme of training. The current pressure on time can restrict development of the possibilities of HEADLAMP.

Programme quality is crucially important, and the issues of quality assurance and quality control emerged as concerns for a number of respondents. Newly appointed headteachers need and deserve the security of knowing that provision and providers are subject to monitoring and evaluation by both the TTA and the programme's participants, and that participants have access to the outcomes of quality assurance processes. In order to improve the effectiveness of the programme, it is essential that the TTA strengthens its guidance to assist headteachers and their governing bodies to link skilled and objective personal and institutional needs analysis with provision of high quality, from a range of well-evaluated providers, over a time-scale that allows flexible and efficient use of the funding available. Headteachers require a clear idea of the status of HEADLAMP tasks and abilities in relation to national standards for school leadership. Further research is also required to investigate the impact of the programme on the effectiveness of school leaders in the early stages of headship.

LEADERSHIP PROGRAMME FOR SERVING HEADTEACHERS

The Leadership Programme for Serving Headteachers was devised as a result of consultation on the NPQH and builds on the considerable work already done in this area by OfSTED, schools, LEAs, HEIs and other agencies. The standards for headteachers also reflect the considerable work undertaken on management standards by those outside the education profession.

The TTA developed the LPSH in partnership with Hay–McBer and its associates, the National Association of Headteachers and the Open University. Business in the Community ensures that each participant is linked to a senior business partner to work on general issues of leadership and management.

Trials were completed in 1999 and the programme is now ready for implementation nationally. The TTA reports that the response of the trials' participants has been enthusiastic, particularly in welcoming the focus on leadership, school improvement and the individual diagnostic information available to each participant.

THE FUTURE

The Green Paper (DfEE 1998b) includes further comments on the professional development of headteachers, here summarised as follows:

The Role of the Head

As stated in earlier chapters the government considers that the headteacher is the key to a school's success. It believes that every school needs a leader to create a sense of purpose and direction, to set high expectations of staff and pupils, focus on improving teaching and learning, monitor performance and motivate the staff to give of their best. Furthermore, the best heads have leadership skills comparable to those of the best leaders in any other sector, including business. The government considers the challenge to be that of creating rewards, training and support of a quality sufficient to attract, retain and develop the skills of many more school leaders of this calibre.

The government's reform programme is extending the funding and responsibility delegated to schools. The reforms are designed to attract talented leaders by giving them the freedom to manage and allocate resources in accordance with school priorities. In return, all schools will be accountable. For schools demonstrating consistent success, the government will provide increased freedom, including the possibility of a new 'light touch' inspection system. For schools performing with less success, new arrangements set out in the School Standards and Framework Act will ensure that they receive, as early as possible, the challenge and support necessary for improvement.

The government recognises (DfEE 1998d) that the challenge of headship can be both rewarding and isolating. Heads require close links internally with senior colleagues and with the chair of the governing body. The government considers that they also need an outside perspective, and that leadership training will help to provide this, as will involvement in local networks such as Partners in Leadership which is run by Business in the Community and the TTA.

A Broader Leadership Group

While heads are of crucial importance, the government acknowledges (DfEE 1998b) that leadership in schools is often shared. Studies have shown that the ability to broaden leadership to embrace several schools is a character-istic of successful heads. In many schools members of senior management teams will help heads give strategic direction in schools. The government believes that governing bodies should have the discretion to reflect the value of such contributions by senior managers by appointing key senior staff to a new leadership pay spine, subject to terms and conditions similar to those which currently apply to heads and deputies.

The government has stated (DfEE 1998d) its intention to encourage faster promotion to headships for the most able. It intends to introduce a fast-track to headship to let promising teachers take modules of the head-ship qualification, by way of preparation. This option would be open to any teachers who were identified in appraisal as promising candidates. It would not be confined to those on the new fast-track route, although the govern-ment hopes fast-track teachers would continue to develop as rapidly in mid-career as in their early years in the profession.

A National College for School Leadership

To underline its commitment to improving the quality of school leadership, the government proposes to establish a National College for School Leadership (DfEE 1998d) which is to combine high-quality educational content with the best in public- and private-sector management. It will have close links with leading business schools and a site of a prestige commensu-rate with its importance, with the highest quality ICT facilities. It will also have a virtual presence on the National Grid for Learning, so that all leaders and aspiring leaders can take advantage of its resources. With its prospectus issued early in 1999, the college is to be in operation by September 2000 (Green 1999).

The government envisages (DfEE 1998b) the main function of the college to be to provide a location for national residential courses relating to all three headship programmes. It will work with the network of regional leadership centres, which the government expects to continue their provision of leadership training. University links could enable the college to be an awarding body for academic qualifications in education. It may also award *associate*, *fellow* and – exceptionally – *companion* status to headteachers at the respective stages of development. The college will provide a nexus where school leaders meet their peers from different regions in the UK and internationally. It will provide sabbaticals for talented serving heads and will commission, across industry and education, research activity relevant to raising standards in schools (Sebba 1999). It could also offer advice on potential career paths, so that heads have a clear sense of the options available.

The impact on standards in schools which the National College for School Leadership has is to be open for scrutiny by the government and by educationalists.

SUMMARY

This chapter has provided an introduction to the government's training programmes for school leaders. The government intends to extend these initiatives. It considers that the existing programmes have proved their worth and proposes to develop them into a national training framework for headship with three levels:

1 qualification, through the National Professional Qualification for Headship which the government proposes should be mandatory by 2002, for all those coming new to headship;
2 induction, to consolidate the skills of new heads;
3 extension, to refresh the skills of experienced heads.

In addition to their own training, headteachers are responsible for the training of others.

The following chapter considers the relationship between schools and professional development. Practical advice is also provided.

Part III

WHOLE-SCHOOL DEVELOPMENT

The focus now changes to the mechanisms for practice in the management of professional development in schools. Each of the next four chapters provides readers with opportunities to reflect on practical implications for their own school. Insight is afforded about what is required, and what works, in achieving high-quality professional development.

Chapter 8 places individual and organisational development within the context of the school development plan (SDP) and provides guidance on creating a policy for professional development within a learning organisation.

Chapter 9 focuses on the management and implementation of appraisal within schools as learning organisations. Government policy, legislation and practical issues are considered, and the importance of basing appraisal on good practice that brings together school and individual needs is emphasised.

Chapter 10 focuses on middle management, an area of professional development that has, until recently, been neglected by school managers and the government. The roles of middle managers are introduced and described, and guidance is given on the development of good practice in schools.

Chapter 11 examines the diverse opportunities for professional development in schools, which encompass: induction; mentoring; self-development; team development; in-house courses; job-exchanges; management development; and consultancy.

Finally, Chapter 12 addresses the challenge of the government's proposed introduction of performance management in schools.

INTRODUCTION

The practical application of management theory to the school context and the implementation of government policies provides the framework for the management of professional development in schools. This is related to the purpose of education, which is to provide tuition and learning opportunities for each member of the school community. Within this context, schools as learning organisations have opportunities to develop their teachers in order to improve standards in the classroom, while motivating them through the provision of career-enhancing openings. There is a danger that, without professional development, teachers will remain rooted in the professional practice that characterised their own experience as both pupils and trainee teachers.

In practice, improving schools require improving teachers. The government has recognised this, as have governors and senior managers in schools. The management of professional development as a resource provides schools with opportunities to develop teachers within the workplace. The identification of what is available for the development of teachers is central to improving schools. Planning for the provision of training requires recognition of the interdependence of school needs and individual needs and the importance of this dual focus for the management of professional development cannot be overstated.

The appraisal process provides the opportunity for teachers to identify strengths and weaknesses, as perceived by themselves and by others. The appraisal process is in part a means for the agreement of individual developmental targets. A professional development co-ordinator should work with both the appraisers and the subjects of appraisal in order to determine the needs of the latter and their satisfaction through training provision. Placed within the programme of professional development activities, individual needs may be addressed by provision that is internal or external to the school.

If managed creatively, professional development can be integral to a teacher's practice – not a distraction from the classroom, but a means of embracing and enhancing good practice. The opportunities described in Part III will hopefully encourage readers to reflect on their own context and the possibilities open to them.

8

THE SCHOOL DEVELOPMENT
PLAN

INTRODUCTION

Planning is of critical importance to the effective management and implementation of professional development programmes, and it is essential that managers and professional development co-ordinators have a thorough understanding of the place of planning in effective management. This chapter considers individual and organisational professional development in the context of whole-school plans. The chapter will consider also the interrelationship of planning and the effective management of professional development in schools.

Effective management may be construed as a three-stage cycle: planning, action and review, as shown in Figure 8.1.

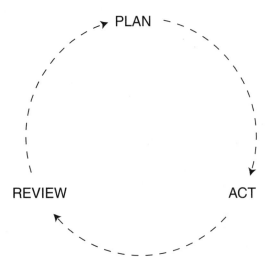

Figure 8.1 The management cycle
Source West-Burnham (1994)

Each plan will encompass

1   Objectives: the goals which are to be achieved, defined in terms suffi-
    ciently detailed and precise to enable others to ascertain whether or not
    they have been achieved.
2   Actions: specification of the activities required to meet the objectives.
3   Resources: identification of the physical resources required to achieve
    the objectives, the personnel to undertake the activities and the time
    scale for completion.

To elaborate: there are planning stages which serve to avoid 'going round in
circles' as consideration is given to the varied combinations of objectives,
actions and resources that provide the way forward. These stages are detailed
in Figure 8.2.

Objectives	**Stage 1**	*Define the objectives*	What are you aiming to achieve?
	Stage 2	*Generate and evaluate objectives / actions*	What are the courses of action available? Which one will best achieve your objectives?
Actions	**Stage 3**	*Identify the actions*	What is required to implement your objectives?
	Stage 4	*Sequence the actions*	What is the best order?
Resources	**Stage 5**	*Identify the resources*	What resources are required?
Review	**Stage 6**	*Review the plan*	Will it work? If not return to stage 2 or 3.
Preparation	**Stage 7**	*Prepare plans and schedules*	Who will do what and when?
Audit	**Stage 8**	*Monitor and evaluate*	Re-plan if necessary.

Figure 8.2   Planning stages
Source Blandford (1997a)

Figure 8.3 presents an alternative view of the planning process. Co-ordinators and senior managers should

1 Define policy and aims – the starting point.
2 Conduct an audit of existing practice.
3 Construct an operational plan.
4 Delineate specific actions to achieve targets.
5 Devise the criteria for evaluation.
6 Implement the planned actions.
7 Check on progress – celebrating success.
8 Review and evaluate the planning process.

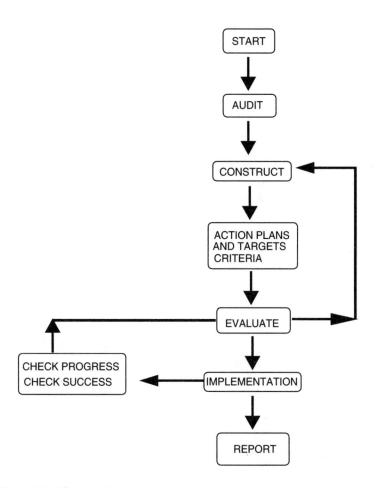

Figure 8.3   The planning process
Source Blandford (1997a)

Participation and Decision-Making

As the above illustrates, planning involves decision-making, at both the individual and collaborative levels. If planning is to be effective, the teachers involved must understand how to prioritise and how to make decisions. According to Warwick (1983)

> Decision-making is so much part of daily life in any school that it can easily be taken for granted. Only when things go wrong, when bad decisions have been taken or the consultation process has broken down, do most teachers become aware of it.

Decision-making is intimately bound up with each manager's personal values, individual goals and management style. In order to make quality decisions Hall and Oldroyd (1990a) suggest that managers should have

- clear personal values
- clear personal goals
- problem-solving skills
- high creativity
- high influence

Managers will need to develop the abilities required to determine when to act on their own or when to collaborate with others. Adopting a structured approach to decision-making will aid the process in determining:

1   A clear analysis of the educational purpose in relation to

- context
- resources
- outcomes

2   A clear specification of the criteria for decisions regarding professional development as determined by

- education development plans
- school development plans
- LEAs
- national standards for teachers
- the Standards Fund
- appraisal and performance management
- department development plans

3   Systematic research

4 Testing decisions (including inspection criteria) against likely outcomes for the quality of teaching and learning

Teams

In schools where performance is improving it is often the case that a collaborative approach is discernible at the senior management level and that such teamworking is replicated among the teaching staff. In such improving schools, staff development tends to be given a high profile, being viewed as an important means of introducing innovation and sustaining curriculum development. While the school improvement literature has emphasised the merits of teachers collaborating and working together as teams (Lieberman, 1986; Rosenholtz 1986; Fullan and Hargreaves 1992; Stoll and Fink 1992), their realisation in practice often proves more difficult to achieve.

The timing of the decision to consult a team will affect

- the quality of the decision;
- staff acceptance of the decision;
- the amount of time involved in the decision-making process.

In schools which demonstrate improvement staff development tends to be viewed in terms not so much of meeting individual needs as of a collaborative endeavour with a whole-school focus. In such schools, staff development is viewed in relation to the overall framework and realised through a whole-school commitment to improvement. In such schools individual teachers are encouraged to be learners themselves, to be coached by their managers and to collaborate by learning with and from each other.

Strategic and Operational Plans

Schools' strategic and operational plans provide the parameters within which their professional development goals can be achieved, and may be summarised as follows:

Strategic planning

If continuing professional development is to be effective it has to relate theory to practice and provide a framework for action that will improve and develop the management of staff in the school. The school as a whole has a responsibility to develop policies and provide resources for staff development – a responsibility, that is, to plan strategically.

A strategy is a broad statement which relates the overall approach and direction to the achievement of personal or organisational targets. Strategic planning is long-term planning which takes into consideration the strengths and weaknesses of the organisation and such external factors as government directives. Developing and maintaining a strategy involves establishing a framework within which an operational plan can take place. Figure 8.4 illustrates the process of designing a professional development strategy.

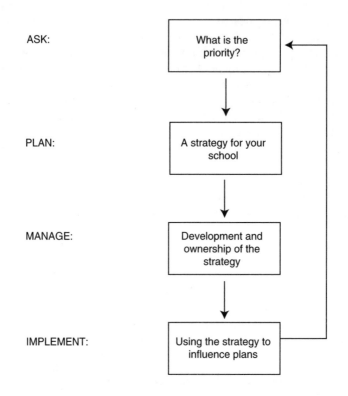

Figure 8.4   Designing a professional development planning strategy
Source Blandford (1998b)

Operational planning

Operational planning is about tasks and targets, and directly relates to the roles of a school's teachers and managers – to who does what, when and how. It is concerned with making things happen within a defined time: how to run a department or team over a short duration, say up to twelve months. Operational planning is detailed. It aims to achieve a particular set of objectives within a given time. A school or departmental development plan is an operational plan.

To be implemented successfully, operational plans for staff development programmes must be headed by the senior management team. Operational plans should set clear and specific objectives for each developmental activity with responsibility allocated to those involved.

It is important that operational plans reflect and inform policy. The process should involve

(a) an evaluation brief that will inform policy;
(b) a statement of aims;
(c) a list of performance indicators relating to targets or outcomes that are *s*pecific, *m*easurable, *a*ttainable, *r*elevant and *t*ime-limited, *in*formative, *e*valuative and *s*timulating;
(d) detailed questions related to the above;
(e) information related to practice arising out of the evaluation process;
(f) outcomes that are accessible to all staff;
(g) conclusions that will inform policy.

LINKING SCHOOL DEVELOPMENT AND PROFESSIONAL DEVELOPMENT

As we saw in Chapter 1, prior to any planning there is a need to address the tension between the institutional and individual requirements of professional development. In planning professional development, any school will need to consider both its own needs as an institution and the aspirations of the individuals who work within it. On many occasions, the two elements will overlap. Only rarely will differences in priorities need to be accommodated.

A recurring claim of this book is that the planning of staff development should relate to the development of the school. Senior and middle managers therefore should consider staff development when setting targets for school development. Targets identified in both plans will need to be considered in parallel.

All schools are required to have a school development plan (SDP). Each SDP will be unique in some aspects, reflecting the culture of the particular school as a learning organisation. The SDP provides a framework for strategic planning in which staff can identify long- and short-term objectives. A SDP should relate clearly to the strategic plan – the school's vision or mission. The strategic plan will focus on long-term whole-school issues, whereas the SDP will focus on short- and medium-term targets (achievable within twelve months) and contribute to the fulfilment of strategic aims that encompass professional development.

The format will vary from one school to another. The SDP may provide

- a demonstration of involvement;
- a focus for action;
- a means of presenting the plan;
- a link to staff development;
- a means of assessing progress.

Figure 8.5 provides an example of a School Development Plan applicable to primary and secondary schools.

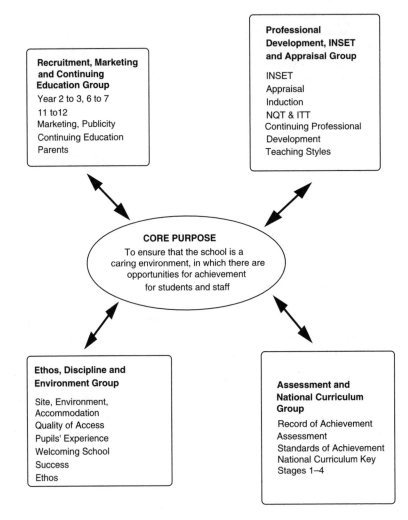

Figure 8.5 Framework for a school development plan
Source Blanford (1997a)

In this example professional development is shown as feeding into and out of the core purpose, relating to both pupils and staff. Professional development is shown to include

- appraisal
- induction
- ITT
- training for NQTs
- teaching styles
- INSET

This framework emphasises the importance of professional development in relation to teaching. In a school guided by this SDP framework the staff, having been given the opportunity for training and development, would feel themselves to be valued contributors to the school's core purpose development (CPD).

Ideally, professional development and school development would be determined and planned together. As McMahon et al. (1999) found, senior managers have become increasingly aware of the tensions that exist between individual and whole-school needs. Figure 8.6 illustrates the relationship between school and professional development in equilibrium. Each process begins with an audit of practice and need, achieved through the school's auditing and appraisal procedures. Targets are then set based on identified needs; this leads in turn to policies, planning and resourcing. Documentation recording policies, procedures and practices, the SDP, and CPD–INSET programmes are then compiled. Action plans provide the detail, identifying what needs to happen, who initiates what, and when. The cycle is completed by monitoring, evaluation and review.

Figure 8.6 indicates also that school improvement will not happen unless professional development embraces both whole-school and individual needs. The practical acknowledgement of this principle is crucial to the management of the effective and improving school.

In sum, a professional development plan would encompass

(a) systems for identifying the training needs of both teaching and support staff;
(b) systems for the communication and dissemination of staff development provision;
(c) systematic evaluation of professional development to inform processes of development planning;
(d) flexibile training service provision;
(e) full involvement of the staff development co-ordinator;
(f) external initiatives;
(g) fostering a culture of lifelong learning;

(h) monitoring staff development provision;
(i) evaluating outcomes to determine the impact of staff development on research, teaching and administration;
(j) attention to the dissemination of outcomes and to follow-up activities to sustain the momentum of training, broaden expertise and to share good practice.

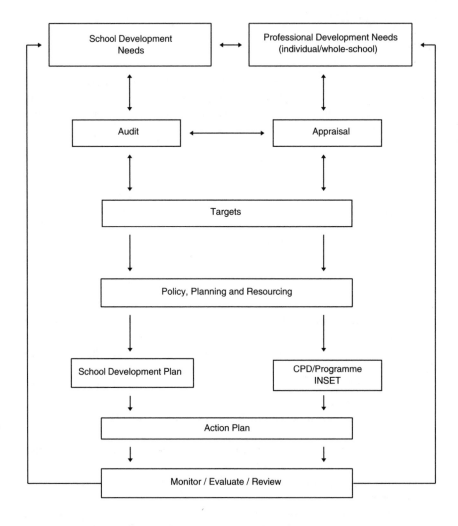

Figure 8.6 The relationship between school and professional development
Source Blandford (1998b)

THE PROFESSIONAL DEVELOPMENT POLICY

A plan for the implementation of professional development would begin with a policy document. The professional development policy would reflect a school management team's desire to value and support its staff. A useful model for the design of a professional development policy, presented by Isaac (1995), utilises the Management Charter Initiative (MCI) Standards as a framework for practice in schools.

Manage policy	Review, develop and present school aims, policies and objectives
	Develop supportive relationships with pupils, staff, parents, governors and the community
Manage learning	Review, develop and implement means for supporting pupils' learning
Manage people	Recruit and select teaching and non-teaching staff
	Develop teams, individuals and self to enhance performance
	Plan, allocate and evaluate work carried out by teams, individuals and self
	Create, maintain and enhance effective working relationships
Manage resources	Secure effective resource allocation
	Monitor and control use of resources

If staff development is to be central to school improvement and effectiveness the professional development policy should be designed by a team the members of which represent all levels of activity within the school. The team would require the ability to plan effectively, as described earlier in this chapter. An effective and improving school will have clear policies relating to the management of learning, people and resources. Personal and professional development are directly related to school development. Each school will need to have a professional development policy that defines aims and describes how these will be implemented.

A professional development policy would include details of

- staff development targets related to school development targets;
- individual needs, as identified by the appraisal process;
- training opportunities via in-school, LEA and national initiatives; award-bearing courses; and whole-school INSET provision;
- resources available – in-school; funding agencies; external bids.

Once needs have been identified, each school has to plan, implement and evaluate a CPD programme. The model is comprehensive and applicable to both primary and secondary schools. An organisational learning culture is vital to the effective implementation of the professional development policy. Important ingredients of an environment appropriate to CPD are

- a positive attitude towards continuing professional development, i.e. lifelong learning;
- awareness, particularly among new practitioners during ITE, of the importance of continuing learning, and, ideally of a synthesis of initial and continuing education;
- to give practitioners the ability to learn effectively, i.e. by applying the knowledge of cognitive psychologists to the needs of the practitioner and professional development: learning, irrespective of the learner's age, is about learning to learn rather than simply being taught;
- expert support and guidance on professional development issues for all parties, especially practitioners.

In conclusion, when preparing a policy, managers should reflect on the choices available within the context of staff-development, identifying:

- what is required to improve performance;
- how this will be done;
- when this will be done.

The General Teaching Council (1993) produced a useful summary of the statements one could expect to encounter in a professional development policy:

- The ultimate aim is to improve the quality of teaching and learning. The immediate aim is to improve the performance of those with school management and teaching responsibilities.
- The programme balances the needs of individuals with whole-school developmental needs.
- The sets of needs to be balanced are: needs of headteachers, senior staff and teachers; needs arising from school development plans; needs of the LEA – subject and management; requirements of LEA policy; requirements of government policy.

PRACTICE

Schools in which the management team is aware of the tension that exists between individual professional development and institutional development are in a position to identify and address key issues. In doing so these schools become self-developing schools, with targets that provide adequate time, resources and follow-up support for staff development. Professional development in the self-developing school will

- emphasise the development of the individual within the school's organisational context and address both individual and organisational needs;
- be congruent with other developments and relate to the whole-school context;
- provide opportunities which are the result of collaboration, participation and negotiation.

The model shown in Figure 8.7 is based on American practice (NPBEA 1993). It illustrates the process of school development planning, applicable to both primary and secondary schools, which emphasises staff development. The model starts with the roles and aims of the school, as given in its mission and vision statements. The school development plan has a supporting professional development policy that includes the appraisal process. The model also indicates how staff development responds to government, LEA, and school goals in order to improve the curriculum, and teaching and learning. Crucially staff development is shown to provide for personal and professional growth and to identify and rectify unsatisfactory performance.

As an operational plan, the model highlights the importance of setting objectives, assigning responsibilities, enlisting participation, providing incentives, and allocating resources for the scheduling and planning of professional development activities. The model concludes with a section on implementation, impact on practice and the need to monitor and evaluate, revise and adapt.

MONITOR, EVALUATE AND REVIEW

In most schools, the monitoring of INSET and the evaluation of its effectiveness and impact on classroom practice remains unsystematic. OfSTED (1997) found that the arrangements for, and evaluation of the impact of, staff development were adequate in most secondary schools, but weak in 25 per cent, a rather higher proportion than in primary schools. Even where monitoring is undertaken, few schools use the results to inform their future planning. Too little attention is given to the impact such training has on classroom practice and on the raising of standards, and arrangements for dissemination of outcomes are generally unsatisfactory.

OfSTED (1997) advises that schools should consider

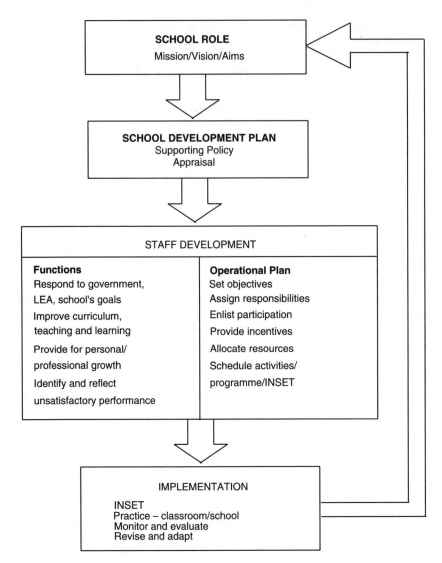

Figure 8.7   Planning staff development
Source Blandford (1998b)

- how to monitor INSET provision more closely and systematically;
- how they might evaluate INSET to determine its impact on improving subject teaching and raising the standard of pupils' achievements;
- giving greater attention to dissemination and follow-up activity to sustain the momentum of training, to broaden expertise and to share good practice;
- making IT an INSET priority: teachers require sufficient familiarity with a range of IT facilities and the skills to apply these in the teaching of their subject;
- teachers and support assistants' INSET needs concerning provision for pupils with special educational needs, in order to develop their expertise in the delivery of the teaching programmes devised for individual pupils.

OfSTED's recommendations reflect the conviction that professional development will be successful only with effective monitoring, evaluation and review procedures. In practice, professional development requires continuous dialogue between managers and teachers. This is an increasingly important aspect of the role of all professional development coordinators (Day 1993b), but it is very difficult to carry through, given limited time and money. OfSTED's comments indicate the importance also of ICT in education.

The processes of monitoring, evaluating and reviewing professional development initiatives now require consideration.

Monitoring

Monitoring is an essential stage in the planning process. Having implemented a plan, managers need to monitor its progress. If plans are not monitored, it will not be possible to determine whether objectives have been achieved. Monitoring will also enable managers to obtain the best results from the available resources. The process enables professional development co-ordinators to work towards agreed objectives. Monitoring is made easier if objectives are clear, practicable and agreed by all members of the team.

Once objectives are agreed, the co-ordinator can move forward with confidence. From clear objectives comes a sense of purpose. Co-operation and agreement when deciding on specific objectives may be less easily obtained.

By measuring and comparing performance against agreed criteria monitoring provides the basis for reflecting on practice. Monitoring will provide an insight into the strengths and weaknesses of professional development policies and programmes. Most significantly, monitoring will provide a framework in which *staff* can reflect on their own practice, one likely outcome of which is enhanced job satisfaction.

As monitoring is an ongoing process it is important, as Hargreaves (1995) has observed, that educational planning by school leaders regularly takes account of the answers to two questions:

1   Who is monitoring what, in which ways and with what effectiveness?
2   Who is responsible for adjusting what, in which ways, when and with what effectiveness?

Figure 8.8 illustrates the place of monitoring within a plan, and emphasises that regular progress reports are required. Progress checking is not something that should be left to the end of the year: monitoring the steps taken to meet aims and objectives in schools should be a constant activity.

In practice, information produced by monitoring will enable schools to follow the scheduled implementation of the professional development policy. Data yielded by monitoring will include:

• operational information
• financial information
• information on performance

Key questions to address here are:

• Who monitors the school in action?
• How is the monitoring carried out?
• How are the governors [and the parents] kept informed?
• Who prepares the final report?

For operational and financial information, professional development co-ordinators will need to regularly monitor actual expenditure and operations

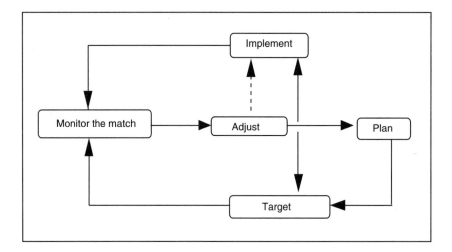

Figure 8.8   Development planning feedback loop
Source Hargreaves (1995)

and to take corrective action against any projected over- or under-spending. A professional development co-ordinator will need to assess the relationship between individual needs (appraisal targets) and school aims (SDP). Resources should be allocated appropriately and plans monitored according to the most beneficial use of internal and external expertise.

Finally, monitoring is an ongoing process of assessing needs, gathering information, communicating and recording progress against agreed targets, in relation to

- the school development plan
- resources – funding arrangements
- internal expertise
- external agents
- LEA initiatives – education development plan
- government initiatives

Evaluation

While monitoring is an ongoing process of checking progress, evaluation is an overall check on whether objectives are achieved within the planned timetable. Like monitoring, evaluation should be a collaborative activity. Evaluation should focus on achievements as well as areas that require improvement. In practice, accountability – both external and internal – is central to educational and management practice in schools. The appraisal of teachers' performance is a key tool in the evaluation process, and the introduction of job descriptions and school curriculum policies has given teachers a clearer definition of their role with which to evaluate their position in the school.

Evaluation is a component of development planning and a prerequisite for the preparation of any subsequent plan. The purpose of evaluating plans is to establish:

- the extent to which the plan has been implemented;
- the extent to which the school's aims have been furthered;
- the impact of the plan on pupils' learning and achievement.

Effective evaluation facilitates the process of recording and reporting to the school leadership on the attainment of targets specified in the SDP.

Hall and Oldroyd (1990b) have neatly outlined the evaluation process in terms of three activities

- asking *questions*
- gathering *information* and
- forming *conclusions*

which are undertaken for the purpose of formulating appropriate *recommendations*.

In contrast to monitoring, evaluation encompasses reviewing the status of a plan's objectives. Through the evaluation process, managers will determine the need to change objectives, priorities and practices. Readers should note the importance of evaluation in enhancing the professional judgement of teachers. Evaluation can lead to a change in teachers' perception of their practice. For co-ordinators, the evaluation of key stage, year or professional development plans can provide the basis for action. Figure 8.9 presents guidelines for the evaluation of practice.

The final stage in the evaluation process is to write a report. The co-ordinator should provide a written report on the evaluation of the professional development policy and programme. An evaluation report might present its information under such headings as

1 Purpose
2 Context
3 Content
4 Process
5 Outcomes

Before disseminating the report, each stage will need to be scrutinised and edited to ensure that only necessary and relevant information is presented.

Review

The review is a consideration of the effectiveness of the school's professional development plan within a wider context. Its focus will be to consider how effective the school's professional development provision has been during the period under review in enhancing the personal and professional lives of its teachers. The key question underlying the review process should be: *What does staff development bring to a professional career?*

If a school is to see itself as a learning organisation, staff will need to feel valued by their managers. Assisting them in their training and development is one way in which managers can achieve this. The review process should reflect this core aspect of professional development in practice.

SUMMARY

Planning is crucial to the effective management and implementation of professional development programmes. Managers and professional development co-ordinators require an understanding of the place of planning in effective management. A plan for the implementation of professional development

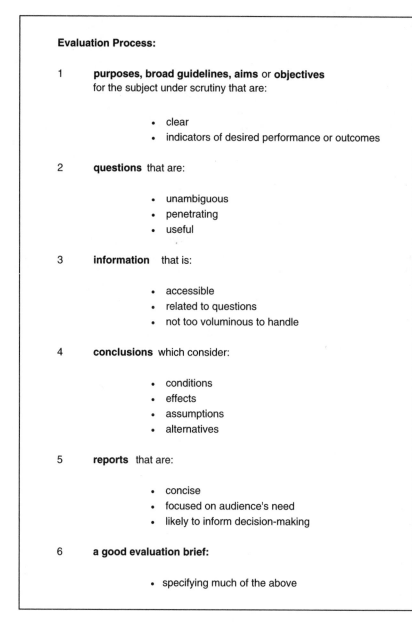

Evaluation Process:

1 **purposes, broad guidelines, aims** or **objectives**
   for the subject under scrutiny that are:

   - clear
   - indicators of desired performance or outcomes

2 **questions** that are:

   - unambiguous
   - penetrating
   - useful

3 **information** that is:

   - accessible
   - related to questions
   - not too voluminous to handle

4 **conclusions** which consider:

   - conditions
   - effects
   - assumptions
   - alternatives

5 **reports** that are:

   - concise
   - focused on audience's need
   - likely to inform decision-making

6 **a good evaluation brief:**

   - specifying much of the above

Figure 8.9 Guidelines for the evaluation of practice

begins with a policy document that should reflect the school management's intention to develop and support its staff.

Prior to any planning, there is a need to address the tension between institutional and individual professional development requirements: the planning of a programme of professional development, in any school, should give balanced consideration to institutional needs and individual aspirations.

School improvement will not happen without professional development for both the individual and the institution. Schools demonstrating improved performance are generally found to have a collaborative team approach at senior management level, an approach that tends to be replicated among the teaching staff. In such schools, staff development is given a high profile, being viewed as an important means of both introducing innovation and sustaining curriculum development.

If staff development is to be central to school improvement and effectiveness, the professional development policy should be produced by a team the members of which are drawn from all levels of activity within the school. Strategic and operational plans provide the parameters within which schools can achieve their professional development goals. In addition, professional development will be successful only when it is subject to effective monitoring, evaluation and review procedures.

Chapter 9 considers the mechanism linking school and individual development – appraisal.

9

APPRAISAL

INTRODUCTION

The function of appraisal within a learning organisation is to provide information on the individual and institutional requirements which, when met, will promote organisation-wide development. Therefore, the importance of appraisal in the context of professional development cannot be overstated. In the school context, as we saw in the previous chapter, the appraisal process is the mechanism that enables practitioners and managers to relate individual targets to school targets.

Appraisal has been a contentious issue in schools since it was first legislated in 1991, following lengthy arbitration between the government and teachers' unions over the period 1982–86. With the publication of the Green Paper (DfEE 1998b) appraisal remains an issue for reform and debate. The original ACAS agreement (1986) on which the pilot schemes were conducted stated that appraisal should be a

> continuous and systematic process intended to help individual teachers with their professional development and career planning and to help ensure that the in-service training and deployment of teachers matches the complementary needs of individual teachers and their schools.

Essentially, appraisal has much to offer schools, though the extent of the benefits of appraisal accruing to a school is to some extent dependent on how well appraisal is handled by school managers. In order to make effective use of appraisal managers must understand both the principles and the process of staff appraisal in relation to professional development. The purpose of this chapter is not to enter the appraisal debate but to present appraisal as an effective means of identifying and fulfilling staff development needs in schools. This chapter will encompass the following: the purpose of appraisal; key elements and outcomes; the appraisal process; and practical issues.

THE PURPOSE OF APPRAISAL

The purpose of appraisal is to motivate and develop individual staff members. Managers will be involved in identifying practitioners' strengths and weaknesses, and setting targets that they are capable of attaining. Appraisal ought *not* to be used to judge individual staff; it a systematic audit or evaluation which leads to performance-related rewards or sanctions, although this point will be reconsidered in terms of what is outlined in the Green Paper (DfEE 1998b) in Chapter 12.

The primary purpose of appraisal is performance enhancement through performance management. One outcome of the appraisal process should be an action plan that identifies specific targets and training needs for the member of staff. If it is to be effective, appraisal must be a developmental process.

Regulation 4 of the National Steering Group's 1991 *School Teacher Appraisal* states that the aim of appraisal is

> to improve the quality of education for pupils, through assisting school teachers to realise their potential and to carry out their duties more effectively.

The statutory aims of appraisal as set out in the 1991 Regulations are:

1   To recognise the achievements of school teachers and help them to identify ways of improving their skills and performance.
2   To help school teachers, governing bodies and local education authorities (as the case may be) to determine whether a change of duties would help the professional development of school teachers and improve their career prospects.
3   To identify the potential of teachers for career development, with the aim of helping them, where possible, through appropriate in-service training.
4   To help school teachers identified as having difficulties with their performance, through appropriate guidance, counselling and training.
5   To inform those responsible for providing references for school teachers in relation to appointments.
6   To improve the management of schools.

Currently, appraisal does not form part of any disciplinary or dismissal procedures, but appraisal statements may be used for the purposes specified in Regulation 14 (National Steering Group 1991), which authorises CEOs or designated officers–advisers to take account of relevant information when taking decisions on promotion, dismissal or discipline and when exercising discretion in relation to pay. In order that a developmental appraisal can survive, continuous evaluation is required of the appraisal process by schools, LEAs, trainers, OFSTED, governing bodies and evaluators.

A working definition of appraisal is of one professional holding him/herself accountable to him/herself in the presence of another professional. As such a staff appraisal scheme should aim to:

- Improve the quality of the education of pupils by assisting staff and headteachers to realise their potential and to carry out their duties more effectively.
- Improve the management of teaching and learning within the classroom.
- Help staff and headteachers identify ways of enhancing their professional skills and performance, and support them in the identification of achievable targets.
- Inform the process of developmental planning within the school.
- Assist in planning the professional development of staff, both individually and collectively, within the framework set by the SDP and with reference to their roles and functions within the school.
- Enhance the overall management of the school.
- Provide opportunities to consider the effective management of change.
- Support the promotion of equality of opportunity for all.

A staff appraisal scheme should be of benefit to members of staff by affording them a better understanding of their jobs, as well as improved feedback and recognition, and by providing them with regular opportunities to consider their professional development needs. Effective appraisal will also contribute to the detail and accuracy of references in support of promotions and job applications, and a greater awareness of career development factors and opportunities. Increased job satisfaction and support for work-related issues will follow from appraisals, which in turn will assist the leadership in co-ordinating school aims and staff aims. Through this process, priorities will be determined and clarified, and roles and responsibilities emphasised. The effective management of professional development will enable school needs to be met through target setting and improved communication, and will engender an environment for the exchange of ideas. Staff appraisal's real value should be discerned in its potential to inform the process of institutional development. In order that it may realise its potential, institutions should aim to have in place a co-ordinated procedure which ensures that mechanisms exist for collating professional development needs identified through appraisal, training needs are related to appropriate staff development opportunities and contingency plans are in place for coping with those whose performance is appraised as poor, whether for personal reasons, e.g. stress, or because of a skill deficiency.

To this end, it is important that

- the process is open and based on a mutual understanding of the context, purpose, procedures, criteria and outcomes of the scheme;

- the scheme's procedures are fair and equitable, and acknowledge equality of opportunity, particularly in relation to gender and race;
- the principles supporting appraisal are acceptable to all staff, the school leadership, governors and LEA personnel, and that all should benefit from participation in the scheme;
- appraisal reflects on the quality of the management of the school;
- the scheme aims to avoid unnecessary and time-consuming administration by maximising available resources, and that it draws on data from a range of sources;
- is integral to the school's development strategy and attempts to balance the demands of professional development with the requirement of public accountability;
- appraisal is deployed with formative intent so that it builds reflectively on experience in support of development and improvement.

Figure 9.1 illustrates the vital relationship of appraisal and professional–school development to school effectiveness. The simplicity of the diagram is somewhat at odds with the complexity of the process.

In practice, appraisal will assist in the planning of staff professional development, individually and collectively, with reference to each person's roles and career plans, within the framework set by the school development plan. This will enhance the overall management of the school and provide opportunities to consider its effectiveness. Effective appraisal will also support the promotion of equality of opportunity.

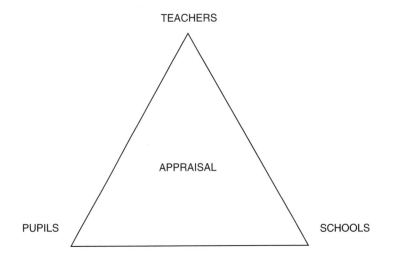

Figure 9.1 Appraisal and effectiveness

PRACTICAL ISSUES

Since the introduction of teacher/headteacher appraisal, many practical issues have emerged, and managers now should give consideration to the following matters when implementing appraisal. It is important to develop trust through a process of consultation with all participants as to the design of the scheme. Care should be taken in the initial presentation of appraisal to staff. A clear statement of aims should be made, as well as of the means of achieving them. Effective training and professional development should be provided to support the scheme, including the use of professional development training days for the appraisers *and* those to be appraised. Specifically, training for appraisers needs to be near the point of implementation and there should be greater emphasis on higher order skills' training. There is also need for an evolving pattern of guidance and documentation by LEAs and the government. Crucially, priority should be afforded to appraisal in the context of the OfSTED inspection system, linking individual targets to school development. Guidelines are required on linking appraisal to school development planning and school effectiveness (see Chapter 8).

Inevitably barriers to the effective management of appraisal have arisen in practice, including the following:

Resources	Time and personnel; funding to support outcomes
Who appraises whom	The selection and allocation of appraisers to practitioners; the involvement of governors; support for the team of appraisers
Timing	Duration of the appraisal cycle
Frequency	No more than one interview per day for those carrying out appraisals
Consistency	Monitoring to ensure continuity between school-based and LEA-based standards
Records and reports	Ownership; duration; accessibility and confidentiality (LEA, governors)
Outcomes	Follow-up; additional support system
Appeals	School system; LEA system

It is important that each of the above is addressed if appraisal is to have successful outcomes.

OUTCOMES

The outcomes of a staff appraisal should be made known and their significance understood. For *members of staff*, these should be:

- fuller understanding of roles;
- improved feedback and recognition;
- awareness of professional development needs;
- increased accuracy of references;
- greater awareness of career development factors and opportunities;
- support for work-related issues;
- greater job satisfaction.

For the *institution*, the anticipated outcomes are:

- raised standards;
- co-ordination of institutional aims and staff aims;
- clarification of the priorities determined;
- greater awareness of roles and responsibilities among staff;
- professional development of management;
- institutional needs addressed through target setting;
- improved communication;
- greater exchange of ideas;
- a more supportive environment.

The success of any appraisal scheme is rooted in identifying aims and objectives, and the planning and determining of the process.

THE APPRAISAL PROCESS

This section provides the reader with checklists to follow when *implementing* appraisal. The management of appraisal requires access to documents relating to:

1   Implementation of the appraisal scheme
   - statement of aims
   - organisation
   - timetable: duration of cycle and frequency
   - scheme documents
   - personnel
   - resources

2   School development plan
   - process/cycle
   - availability and accessibility

3   Job descriptions

4   Equal opportunities' policy
5   Staff development policy
6   Professional development: co-ordination and resources

The detailing of the implementation plan will depend on the definition of the role of the appraisers. Definition will vary between institutions, but the role will include:

- overseeing, co-ordinating and conducting the process of appraisal;
- agreeing, with each practitioner appraised, the specific focus of the appraisal, and what information will be gathered, by what method and from whom (such information should focus on issues, not personality);
- carrying out, and briefly reporting on, classroom observation of the practitioner, using an agreed method of data collection and focusing on the areas identified jointly with the practitioner;
- provide the practitioner, prior to the professional meeting, with a written copy of the information collected (observation, job description);
- setting the date, venue and agenda for the appraisal interview;
- reviewing performance and agreeing targets with the practitioner in the appraisal interview, at which stage professional development opportunities should be considered;
- agreeing a date, time and venue for the follow-up meeting;
- drafting an agreed written summary as a result of the meeting and encouraging the practitioner to follow the action plan agreed;
- adjusting the targets set in the light of changed circumstances;
- monitoring the professional development of the practitioner and consulting with him or her periodically about progress made.

Once the role of the appraiser has been agreed by all staff, a more detailed plan of the process of appraisal is required. The plan is likely to encompass the following:

1   The initial meeting

- the purpose
- date, time and venue for appraisal interview
- date, time and focus of classroom observation
- objectives of the interview
- data collection instruments to be used
- what information is to be collected and from whom
- the information to be made available to practitioners prior to the interview

2 Staff self-appraisal: practitioners to use a prompt sheet to support reflection on his or her role and performance

3 Classroom observation

- specific focus: details of class and groupwork being carried out, teacher's plans and preparation
- questioning techniques
- agreed methodology and format

4 Debriefing following observation: relevant data used to inform discussion, 'teaching analysis' within two weeks

5 Collection of other relevant data, including

- non-teaching pupil-related duties
- curriculum-based evidence
- data compiled during action research
- data relevant to past year's work
- feedback from areas of additional responsibility

6 Requirements for the appraisal interview (one interview only per day per appraiser)

- documents to be shared prior to interview
- clear agenda
- comfortable environment that is free from interruption
- adequate time
- atmosphere of confidentiality and trust
- nature of previous relationships
- high priority by both appraiser and appraised

7 Components of the appraisal

- consideration of job description
- review of work
- identification of expectations
- identification of successes achieved and previous staff development
- professional development needs
- identification of targets, including consideration of likely constraints

8 Preparation of an appraisal statement, which should record

- the practitioner's achievements, successes and elements of good practice
- areas of deficiency and weakness, and suggestions for dealing with them
- requests for help and support
- suggestions for professional development
- comments about matters affecting the individual's work

9   Agreed targets should be

- stated clearly
- in the form of an action plan
- few in number
- challenging but attainable
- subject to monitoring and review
- connected to classroom strategies, school performance, career aspirations and professional development plan

Readers should note that appraisal will also cover the full range of professional duties including temporary responsibilities. The basis of appraisal should be the individual teacher's job description, which should reflect the balance between duties in and out of the classroom. Figure 9.2 illustrates the appraisal cycle.

The cycle:

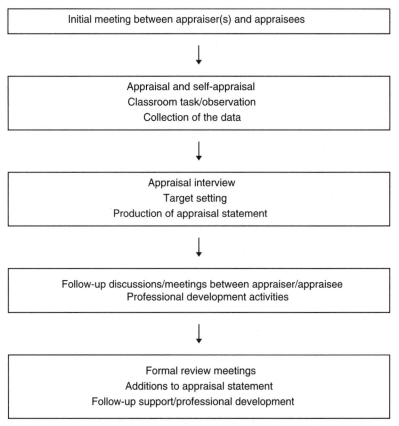

Figure 9.2   The appraisal cycle
Source Blandford (1998b)

Following completion of the appraisal, copies of the appraisal report should be forwarded to the practitioner appraised for his or her agreement, and thereafter to the headteacher. The appraisal report is to be treated as confidential, and permission will be required, even by those with access, before the information can drawn upon in making decisions concerning professional development targets, pay, promotion or disciplinary action.

At a time agreed by the participant and appraiser, a review meeting will be held in order to review progress and consider the appropriateness of targets, professional development, training for career development, and to raise any other issues.

PRACTICAL ISSUES

Generating Job Descriptions for Appraisal

Central to an effective scheme for staff appraisal is the preparation of job descriptions, which will normally be carried out by a manager. Key features of a job description are that it should be jointly discussed and cover all aspects of the individual's work. A job description should state precisely to whom the individual is accountable and be broken down into areas of specific responsibility. It should be open-ended and should support development.

A teacher's job description should include

- appropriate personal details;
- the job title;
- a statement of the primary function of the job, which is clear but brief, and describes the overall role of the job holder;
- a statement of line-management responsibilities and accountability;
- a detailed statement of the main duties, which could be broken down into subsections and which may be used as a checklist to ascertain whether the job-holder's performance is satisfactory;
- a summary of duties.

Job descriptions will be used as part of the appraisal process to check whether the job holder is effective in carrying out all the required functions, and the training or development that would be useful to improve his or her performance.

Writing Job Specifications

A model is useful in undertaking job analyses. What follows is an outline that can be helpfully applied.

1   *Key tasks*
    • What is done?
    • When is it done? – include teaching and managerial details
    • Why is it done?
    • Where is it done?
    • How is it done?

2   *Responsibilities*
    • Responsibility for others – pupils and teachers
    • Responsibility for resources
    • Responsibility for budgets

3   *Working relationships*
    • With superiors
    • With colleagues
    • With other departments and agencies
    • With pupils
    • With parents
    • With team members

4   *Job requirements*
    • Skills and experience
    • Education and training
    • Health
    • Motivation and social skills
    • Personal qualities

5   *Working conditions*
    • The school
    • The department and the team
    • Social conditions
    • Funding and pay

6   *Check up*
    • With the job holder
    • With his or her manager

From the job analysis, a job description can be written. This should describe the job, and the incumbent's responsiblities, functions and duties.

CONDUCTING AN APPRAISAL INTERVIEW

A manager will require training in order to develop the key skills of appraisal interviewing. These skills are listed below.

- Questioning
- Analysis
- Summarising and reflecting
- Clarification
- Giving and receiving feedback
- Problem solving
- Target setting

The kind of information required largely determines the types of question used in the appraisal process. For example:

Open	to encourage another person to explore matters of importance to them
Reflective	to encourage someone to explain his/her feelings or attitudes on an issue
Leading	to guide a person towards an answer which the questioner wants or expects to hear
Hypothetical	to encourage someone to step outside his/her current position, mental set or attitude and consider a matter from another standpoint
Closed	to gather very specific facts or obtain yes–no answers
Probing	to keep the person on the same topic but explore it in more depth

The teacher should be allowed to present information and analysis while the appraiser listens actively and avoids interruption. The skills of active listening involve:

- securing an environment conducive to the kind of interchange required for effective appraisal – appropriate proximity, orientation, posture and gesture;
- getting the subject to talk – inviting and encouraging responses, questioning, knowing when to remain silent, use of eye contact;
- comprehension of spoken thoughts, ideas and feelings;
- paraphrasing and summarising in order to convey to the subject that he or she is understood.

Next the appraiser will present the collected data and discuss its implications with the teacher, encouraging him or her to identify areas for development and possible targets, and conclude with an agreed written statement of the action to be taken.

The appraisal interview will

- involve detailed consideration of the job description of the teacher being appraised;
- review the teacher's work, including successes and areas of prior development, with reference to the data collected and the classroom observation;
- identify and discuss professional development needs and career aspirations, as appropriate;
- discuss the teacher's role in, and contribution to, the management of the school;
- identify any constraints that prevent the teacher from fulfilling his or her role and functions;
- identify targets for future development;
- clarify the points to be made in the appraisal statement.

Classroom Observation

Another key component in the appraisal process is classroom observation. During the observation, it is important for the appraiser to concentrate on the agreed focus of the lesson. He or she should record observations accurately and systematically, while maintaining the agreed relationship with both the pupils and the teacher under observation. It is important that the appraiser is objective and non-judgemental, and that he or she gives a response to the teacher immediately after the lesson. Observation is followed by a feedback session, which should take place as soon after the lesson as possible, in a quiet and informal atmosphere.

A mechanism for feeding back information is illustrated in Figure 9.3, the Jo-Hari Window. The sectors within the frame represent all that is known about us, either by ourselves or by others. Self-awareness is increased when we are successful in penetrating the 'blind' area but also when, through sharing more of ourselves with others, we begin to diminish the 'hidden' area and thereby appreciate the greater potential in our own lives. To increase awareness of ourselves, we need to pursue situations which provide opportunities both for disclosure and for evoking feedback on our own behaviour or performance.

Setting Targets

Target setting is integral to the appraisal process. A target is a statement of intent, agreed by two or more people, which refers to some desired state of affairs to be achieved. Since in most circumstances this is a change involving an improvement of some kind, targets should:

- aim to facilitate the teacher's own professional development;
- be agreed in the context of the school's development plan and organisational goals;
- be feasible and realistic in the light of available resources;
- include some agreed performance indicators to illustrate the extent to which the target is being achieved;
- be few in number;
- define the support afforded in order to help the teacher achieve the target (the appraiser should accept responsibility for ensuring that support is provided);
- be reviewed in the follow-up meetings and modified as necessary.

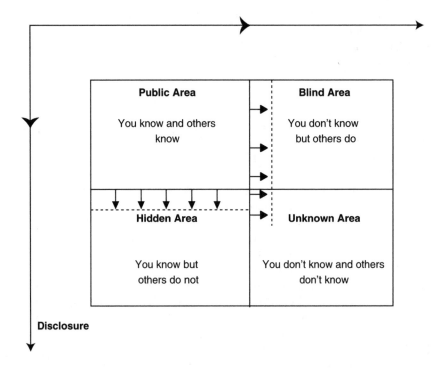

Figure 9.3   The Jo-Hari Window

Agreed targets should be: stated clearly; linked to an action plan; few in number; challenging but attainable; subject to monitoring and review; and relate to raising standards of achievement, classroom and management strategies, school performance, career and professional development.

A guide to setting targets

A useful guide to target setting is SMARTIES:

S   Specific
M   Manageable
A   Appropriate
R   Realistic
T   Time-constrained
I   Informative
E   Evaluated
S   Stimulating

Cardinal Rules of Appraisal

As a conducting checklist, headteachers and deputy headteacher members may find helpful the seventeen 'cardinal rules of appraisal', from the NUT's *Appraisal* (1993a):

1   Make sure that the LEA's appraisal scheme is acceptable to local unions.
2   Demand at least one day's joint training for appraisers and those to be appraised.
3   No appraiser should be responsible for more than four candidates, other than in exceptional circumstances.
4   Well-grounded fear of harassment is a reason for requesting an alternative appraiser.
5   Appraisal should be based on an up-to-date job description.
6   The complete appraisal process should take place in directed time and at appropriate venues.
7   All decisions made at the initial meeting should be based on mutual negotiation.
8   How frank the self-appraisal is will depend on the context of appraisal in the school or LEA.
9   Ensure that classroom observations are promptly followed up.
10 Remember that, in successful appraisal interviews, the candidate should speak for about 80 per cent and the appraiser for 20 per cent of the time.
11 Agreed appraisal targets should help, not hinder, the professionalism of the candidate.
12 The appraisal statements can include the comments of the candidate if they are registered within twenty working days.
13 Because confidentiality must extend to the writing of the appraisal statement, normal secretarial assistance may not be used.
14 In anticipation, or reinforcement, of the LEA's advice to chairs of governors not to ask to see appraisal targets, headteachers should seek to persuade

the chair of governors, from the outset, that such a request would seriously threaten the introduction of appraisal in terms of its being a professional development process. Headteachers, together with teacher governors, have the important task of expressing and justifying at every opportunity opposition to the chair having access to targets, with the aim of ensuring that chairs do not ask to see appraisal targets.

15 Amendments to the appraisal statement or a new appraisal can be demanded by a review officer appointed within the appraisal complaints procedure.

16 For effective appraisal, systematic follow-up action must be pursued by the appraiser and candidate.

17 The review meeting should be used to review the targets set for the individual and their relationship to the overall appraisal process taking place in the school.

THE FUTURE

Appraisal is currently undergoing review within the context of the government's professional development initiatives to raise standards in schools. It is proposed that LEAs will have a particular involvement with schools that are running into real difficulty, but will consult with all schools in the setting of targets as they draw up their educational development plans (EDPs). As indicated in the Green Paper (DfEE 1998b), the DfEE will be publishing a new framework for practice and guidelines, the implementation of which will encompass much of the above.

A key development will be the introduction of appraisal as an annual process. This will provide the opportunity to agree targets with teachers in tandem with targets set by the school in the development plan. Each of these will be influenced by key points for action in OfSTED reports, benchmark information from the national data collected by OfSTED and LEAs' educational development plans.

The developing work of the TTA on professional standards may also lead to agreements about appropriate targets for particular stages in a teacher's career. It is important that any changes to appraisal systems cut down rather than increase bureaucracy and have the improvement of pupils' performance as a constant focus.

On the basis of a more systematic recognition of teachers' achievements, key aspects of the new appraisal system will be:

• the setting of objectives which are clear and measurable, so that appraisers, and candidates know what the priorities are and can assess how far objectives have been met;
• the inclusion of targets relating to pupil performance;

- the assessment of teachers' performance against their objectives in the context of national professional standards and teachers' observed strengths and weaknesses;
- the use of appraisal outcomes to influence pay decisions as well as to inform teachers' further professional development;
- training and support to ensure that those involved know their responsibilities and are able to conduct appraisals fairly.

Classroom Teacher Appraisal

Appraisal of classroom teachers will be based on the teachers' job descriptions and at least three objectives agreed at the start of the appraisal cycle in the context of the school's development plan and national teaching standards. Appraisal will draw on classroom observation and other information about performance gathered in the course of the appraisal cycle as part of the normal process of management, monitoring and evaluation. This will also involve an appraisal interview with a senior manager, at which a teacher's performance is assessed in the light of progress against previously agreed objectives and new objectives are set for the coming year.

The government considers that the evidence to be discussed in appraisal interviews must give a reliable view of performance. Appraisal will not generate a requirement for additional data collection, but will draw on the normal management cycle of monitoring and evaluation. Depending on a teacher's role, relevant data could include:

- records of classroom observation by the line manager and others;
- comparative performance data;
- scrutiny of pupils' work, schemes of work and lesson plans;
- a record of the teacher's professional development, with evidence of its impact on teaching and learning.

Following the annual review meeting, the senior manager will then write an appraisal statement covering three outcomes:

1   An assessment of overall performance, based on achievements against the previous year's agreed objectives, reflecting factors such as the challenge of particular groups of pupils and the level of demand of the teacher's objectives. The statement should summarise the evidence against each objective and highlight particular strengths and weaknesses in performance and outcomes.
2   A new set of objectives defined for the coming year.
3   A plan for professional development activities and other actions designed to support the achievement of the coming year's objectives.

Headteacher Appraisal

The government proposes that the governing body should be responsible for ensuring that the head's performance is properly appraised each year and for taking account of the appraisal outcome in the review of the head's pay. The government believes high-quality independent advice should be available to governing bodies to enable them to perform this function consistently. It recommends that the governing body should make use of an external adviser in setting the head's annual targets and in appraising the head's performance.

At the start of the academic year the head will agree at least three objectives with the governing body, two of which must relate directly to his or her improved performance in the context of school priorities and targets. At least one of the head's objectives should relate to pupils' performance targets for the school; another should address a major school priority for the year, such as reviewing the school's special needs' policy and implementing necessary changes. The government advises that at least one objective should focus on improving professional effectiveness based on the national standards for headteachers.

The head will be responsible for keeping a record of performance from sources such as the outcomes of key-stage assessments and external examinations, benchmarking data and OfSTED reports. The government will expect a school's governing body to designate one of its members for the task of considering, together with the external adviser, the results achieved in terms of the head's objectives and against the national standards.

The appraisal meeting will involve the governing body's representative as well as the external adviser, and will have the following outputs:

1   a report assessing performance in the light of progress against agreed objectives which takes account of their degree of challenge; the report should summarise the evidence against strengths and weaknesses in performance;
2   a new set of objectives for the coming year, agreed between the head, the external adviser – where appropriate – and the governing body;
3   a plan for agreed professional development activities and other actions designed to support the achievement of the new objectives.

The external adviser engaged for the appraisal of the headteacher will support the governing body in assessing the head's performance against his or her own and the school's objectives, and against national headship standards, in suggesting revised objectives and – on request – giving advice to the governing body about the implications of the appraisal outcomes for the headteacher's pay.

Funding

The LEA will be responsible for producing data to support the new appraisal process. The authority will want to consider also the training and support to offer in response to its schools' needs and wishes, taking account of national statutes and guidance on content, and to share good practice to help schools avoid unnecessary bureaucracy.

SUMMARY

This chapter has shown that in practice appraisal will assist in the planning of professional development for staff, collectively and individually, within the framework set by the school development plan and with reference to each person's roles and career plans. Appraisal is the mechanism for linking school and individual targets and should be valued as a system for development.

Appraisal is currently undergoing review within the context of the government's professional development initiatives to raise standards in schools. A key development will be the introduction of appraisal as an annual process, as this will provide the opportunity to agree targets with teachers in tandem with targets set by the school in its development plan. A critique of these proposals can be found in Chapter 12.

Chapter 10 examines a neglected area in the professional development of teachers and middle management. While the process of promotion to key-stage and year headships in schools is clear, there is in contrast a dearth of training opportunities for middle managers. Given the relationship of appraisal to individual and school development, an analysis of middle managers' needs should be prerequisite to the provision of training.

10

MIDDLE MANAGEMENT

INTRODUCTION

Since the Education Reform Act (1988), the role of middle managers in schools has developed into a position encompassing whole-school responsibilities. Recent commentaries (e.g. Doe 1999) have emphasised the need for middle managers to be given further training opportunities. This chapter provides guidance for middle managers about identifying and developing management skills. As the majority of professional development co-ordinators are middle managers, the issue is particularly relevant. Many of the issues raised are pertinent also to the development and maintenance of a learning organisation culture.

The chapter begins with a definition of middle-management roles and responsibilities and an examination of the issues confronting middle management. Guidance is given on team management, and the chapter concludes with recommendations for middle managers' professional development.

WHAT IS SCHOOL MIDDLE MANAGEMENT?

The management of schools has changed significantly since the 1988 Education Reform Act (ERA). All school teams – nursery, primary, special and secondary – now have managers whose responsibilities hitherto were the domain of senior managers or LEAs. The areas of school management in which the greatest impact has been felt are shown in Figure 10.1.

These changes set new parameters for management practice in schools. As a direct consequence of the ERA new structures for the management of schools have evolved which, in turn, have led to new roles for school managers and a proliferation of management teams. In essence, someone needed to do the job! Teachers are no longer classroom managers responsible for the delivery of the curriculum: they are managers with responsibilities as diverse as developing the new school prospectus and purchasing carpets. While teachers' primary functions remain within the context of learning,

Aspect of ERA	Affected area of school management
Local management of schools (LMS)	Budget and staffing
Parental choice	Marketing and development
National Curriculum (NC)	Curriculum co-ordination
League tables	Pastoral and academic
Continuing professional development (CPD)	Staff development, appraisal and selection
School development plan (SDP)	Strategic planning
Diversity	Selection and specialisation

Figure 10.1   The effects of ERA on school management

Source Blandford (1997a)

the profession has been required to develop new skills to accommodate the need to manage policies, resources and people. As Spinks (1990: 121–22) stated:

It follows from continuing developments in devolution of responsibility for decision-making to schools and communities that schools now have three major tasks:

1   the development of a relevant curriculum to meet the needs of the students
2   the development of management skills to deliver the curriculum to students in the most effective and efficient ways possible through the resources available
3   the development of approaches through which to manage change as a natural phenomenon in schools.

In practice, a manager is someone who gets the job done, through people. Everard (1986) defined a manager as one who

• knows what he or she wants to happen and causes it to happen;
• is responsible for controlling resources and ensuring that they are put to good use;
• promotes effectiveness in work done, and a search for continual improvement;
• is accountable for the performance of the unit for which he or she is responsible and of which he or she is a part;
• sets a climate or tone conducive to enabling people to give of their best.

More specifically, the key function of school management is to oversee policy, people and resources in order to create, maintain and develop conditions which enable effective learning to take place. If to manage is to get things done; school management is to get things done within the framework of practice determined by the school as a learning community and organisation.

Certain responsibilities of schools' middle management are generic and apply whether the institution is a small nursery, a primary, secondary or special school, or a large comprehensive school. It follows that the framework for the organisation of one school can be applied to all schools. Differentiation will, however, occur: in the real and 'practical world' which they inhabit (Harrison 1995) managers will make diverse choices as to how their schools will be organised. Essentially middle managers are responsible for the management of people: each framework for practice functions only as a model to be interpreted by individuals.

Middle Management Defined

The structure of school management is changing from the traditional 'top–down' hierarchical arrangement to a flatter model in which the majority of staff will be involved in the management of their school. From this scenario has evolved the middle-management function of overseeing the work of teams. Staff in schools today are typically deployed as members of one or more of a range of teams, including:

- subject teams
- year teams
- curriculum, faculty and department teams
- key-stage teams
- SEN teams

Schools' need of middle managers, as already remarked, arose from the change from LEA- to school-based management. In practical terms, many school managers have found themselves unable to meet the demands of the new management practices introduced since 1988. Throughout the profession, all practitioners are today required to consider management issues as part-and-parcel of their daily practice.

Many schools have created working groups as means of managing change. These working groups have responsibility for the development, implementation and review of school, LEA and government policies.

A teacher is a classroom manager who oversees pupils' acquisition of knowledge and their development of understanding, skills and abilities. The middle manager, on the other hand, is a manager of teams, and oversees the application of the knowledge, understanding, skills and abilities of colleagues. In either role the teacher–manager is required to work with other people. This involves working with individuals' values and beliefs as these are made manifest in the ethos of the school. Middle managers are therefore continually creating, forming and applying practices and policies in order to contribute to their schools' effectiveness.

Team membership and leadership are crucial to school management, and middle managers, who are themselves managed, therefore have their own team roles to perform. The middle manager therefore has contrasting roles within school management teams. Middle management requires individuals to identify, and identify with, different tasks and roles: teacher, leader and team member. This hybrid function within school management provides the framework for the daily practice of the middle manager. Figure 10.2 locates the middle manager as a teacher, leader and team member in the school context.

The effectiveness of middle managers depends on their ability to identify the capacity in which they are required to function at any given moment in the school day. The effective manager will, in practice, identify the appropriate management role required by each situation. It is essential, therefore, that a middle manager quickly comes to terms with the ambivalence of perspective which is characteristic of the role.

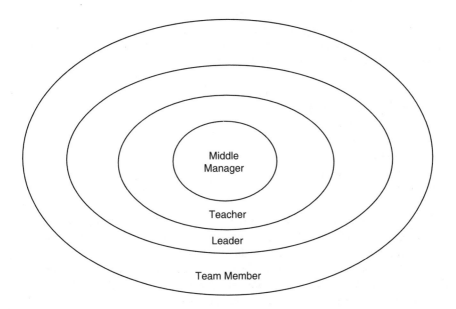

Figure 10.2   Middle management in context
Source Blandford (1997a)

An understanding of whole-school issues is required. What these issues are will be determined by the government, the LEA, the school's senior management team (SMT) and governors. Other agencies will be involved in the daily management of the school: ethnic and crisis support groups; educational welfare and probationary services; educational psychologists; university and other research teams providing academic and management advice; LEA and independent inspection teams; and consultants. A middle manager should know what interests these groups represent, how frequently they visit the school, and their roles within the whole school. There should be no pastoral–academic divide.

Middle Management in Practice

If the school's middle managers are to be effective they will be aware of the need to identify and adopt best practice. The National Commission on Education (NCE 1996: 366) has stated that school effectiveness involves 'leadership, ethos, high expectations of pupils and staff, positive teaching and learning styles, sound assessment procedures, recognition of pupils' participation in learning, parental involvement in the life of the school and a programme of extra-curricular activities'. Rutter et al. (1979) suggested that middle managers should have strong motivational skills to generate staff involvement and a positive school ethos, and should encourage good practice directed towards extending this ethos.

The divisions of responsibility within a school are, in practice, determined by the needs of all pupils to learn and of all teachers to teach. These needs require policies at schools' macro and micro levels, covering:

- assessment and reporting procedures
- professional development
- the curriculum
- learning and teaching styles
- support
- equality of opportunity
- pastoral care

All policies relating to the above will need to be generally available to members of staff. Middle managers need to acquire a thorough understanding of all policies relevant to their practice.

Middle managers also have a role as teachers. On balance, their timetables will have more class-contact hours than will those of colleagues at senior management level. In order to understand the nature of their job, middle managers will need to consider their teaching commitment within the context of their middle-management role. This is an issue not merely of time management but of the congruence of the two roles. If practitioner

166

values and beliefs are transferable to management practice, teaching and middle management may co-exist successfully. If, however, individuals adopt values and beliefs in their management role different from their values and beliefs as practitioners, a less successful outcome may be anticipated. The values espoused by middle managers will largely determine their management style – and the nature of their relationship with colleagues.

The acquisition of the knowledge, understanding, skills and abilities required to manage people takes time. Middle managers should be aware of the importance of reflecting on and learning from their practice, and of constantly evaluating their roles within an institution. This is a two-way process: managers must know themselves and their team members, and the team should know its manager. Inconsistency will lead to bad practice, whereas clarity of direction is respected and valued.

Roles

Being a middle manager does not mean being 'all things to all people'. Middle managers must select and adopt the management style which fulfils the requirements of the post. Knowing what is required is the key. It is essential for middle managers to identify their roles in terms of

- tasks
- responsibilities
- relationships
- working conditions
- external influences

To avoid quandaries middle managers will need to have an understanding of their roles in relation to those of others. Analysing the design of the job, applying this in practice, and reflecting on failures and successes are central to middle management. A middle manager's team will, at times, function as a discrete unit, but can never be separated from whole-school policies. Moreover, the middle manager must be loyal to his or her own leader. 'Empire building' is not an appropriate approach to middle management. An effective middle manager will be able to identify the different influences on his or her function, and the organisational structure of the school should give a clear view of his or her position within the management system.

Middle managers will be subject, too, to influences from outside their remit within the school, such as community and family responsibilities. It is essential that middle managers are able to maintain their personal and social activities outside the school, otherwise their outlook will be limited to a single track.

Essentially middle managers are responsible for

- the implementation of school-wide strategies, structures and intentions, fine-tuning them in the process to suit the real world;
- being role models whose daily behaviour represents to their teams the people-centred culture of the school's organisation;
- the passing on of good practice acquired as a consequence of operational experience and learning.

Brown and Rutherford (1996) provide further insights into the role of middle managers by applying the following descriptions to secondary-school heads of department:

Servant Leader	Serving pupils, teachers and senior management
Organisational Architect	Engaging in professional discussions
Moral Educator	Committed to high educational values
Social Architect	Sensitive to the needs of pupils and staff
Leading Professional	Spending 80 per cent of time teaching in addition to leading their team

In conclusion, middle managers should have an understanding of their roles as detailed in their job descriptions, negotiated with the senior management team and approved by governors. Clarity is essential if middle managers are to avoid the ambivalence which leads to confusion. Resolving management problems early is preferable to watching them grow beyond manageable proportions. In short, the function of the middle manager in schools is threefold:

1   to teach;
2   to lead teams;
3   to work as a team member.

TEAM MANAGEMENT

The size of the department, faculty or teams responsible for each subject area will be based on the size of the school. Formula funding based on pupil numbers will determine the amount of income for each school, and therefore the number of staff. A middle manager responsible for a department or faculty will decide the number of staff in each academic team according to the number of pupils attending the school. The size of the academic team in turn will determine the financial incentive allocated to the post and the extent of delegation possible.

In contrast, the tasks of each academic team do not vary according to size. At each key stage, their functions will be to ensure delivery of the National Curriculum, to see that each pupil is assessed and that reporting criteria are met. The effective functioning of the teams for curriculum support, special needs, language support and music (peripatetic staff) is part of middle management's remit.

Communication, written and oral, is essential for the success of the team. A middle manager will need to be both disseminator and gatherer of information, acting as a 'gate-keeper' for his or her teams; awareness of teams' needs is also important, though middle managers should endeavour not to over-protect their staff.

Given that a middle manager is the central person in a team they will also need to recognise that all teachers have a pastoral responsibility for pupils. However, heads of year manage this area, which involves regular contact with parents, members of the community and external agencies. Areas of responsibility should be well-defined within the management structure of the school. This is occasionally a neglected area within school management.

A framework for the management of pastoral care should (as the above indicates)

- be workable;
- recognise the needs of the school;
- be understood and acknowledged by all staff;
- relate to the school's vision and mission;
- allow middle and senior managers to develop knowledge and understanding, skills and abilities;
- allow middle managers to participate in continuing professional development (CPD) programmes.

Conflict of roles

Many teachers regard involvement in team management as undesirable. Whether as a consequence of their own experiences of poor management or because they believe that management and teaching are not compatible, such teachers prefer to teach and leave management to others.

Middle managers may encounter management dilemmas which generally arise out of the conflict between management of learning and management of people. Hall and Oldroyd (1990a: 38) identified role strain as a difficult area. Sources of role strain were considered to be:

Role ambiguity	When you are unclear about what is expected
Role conflict	When one of the roles you have is in conflict with another
Role overload	When more is expected of you in a role than you can manage
Role underload	When you feel under-utilised in your role

A means of addressing these issues is to establish what the job involves, and this is illustrated in Figure 10.3.

Player–Managers

Middle managers in schools are very much player–managers, participating in the daily tasks of teaching while fulfilling the role of team leader or manager, indicating the importance of flexibility required of a middle manager in relation to both leaders and teams. School middle managers are led by line managers (depending on where the job is in the management

Area

- leadership
- participation and delegation
- stress management
- conflict management
- knowledge of schools as organisations
- communication: interpersonal relationships
- understanding of teams
- time management
- appraisal
- strategic planning
- operational planning
- decision-making
- monitoring and evaluation
- financial management
- management of change
- staff development
- recruitment and selection
- self-evaluation

Figure 10.3 What the job involves

structure), the senior management team, the governing body and by advisory and inspection teams.

There is a distinctive status to being a manager, and identifying what this means early on in one's management career is important. Equally, there is a status attached to team membership. Almost all middle managers will join teams that have responsibility for the management of the school. For example, if appointed to the post of head of Year 8, you may be invited to join the school's pastoral team, in which case your role as a player–manager could be represented schematically as shown in Figure 10.4.

It is therefore essential for middle managers to know their roles, their teams and their line managers. Crucially, this includes an understanding of their own needs and capabilities and of those of the others involved. Middle managers should be able to identify the relevance of information for those who lead and those who are led. The role of the middle manager is thus essentially a hybrid.

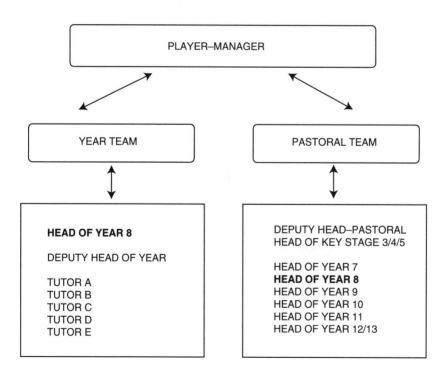

Figure 10.4 The player–manager's role

Source Blandford (1997a)

Managing Professional Development

School and staff development are also the responsibility of middle managers in primary and secondary schools. In the context of departmental, year group, key-stage or pastoral team development, the identification of professional development needs and opportunities is an important function of the middle manager. The middle manager's responsibility for team development is shown in Figure 10.5, which illustrates how the team leader's ability to identify and communicate team needs and development opportunities will impact on school development.

Figure 10.5 also indicates that the process of planning for key-stage, year, subject or department teams is itself developmental. Such initiatives will provide middle managers with opportunities to develop planning, team-building and management skills.

Career Development for Middle Managers

Heads of department and curriculum leaders are positioned to be major forces in driving improvement in standards of teaching. The government believes (DfEE 1998b) that schools should recognise the importance of their contribution in the allocation of training budgets. Introductory leadership and management courses from the headship training programme should be made available to teachers taking on management responsibilities for the first time, whether or not headship is ultimately their aim. Successful teachers can also gain – and contribute – valuable experience working on a part-time or seconded basis in their LEA's advisory services.

An example of professional development for middle managers is provided by the NEAC's assessment of competence programme. The programme involves participants for one full day. NEAC assesses competences – the skills and abilities needed for successful leadership in education. The chosen competences, which have been extensively researched, fall into four groups:

Administrative	Problem analysis; judgement; organisational ability and decisiveness
Interpersonal	Leadership; sensitivity; stress tolerance
Communication	Oral communication; written communication
Personal	Interests and motivation; educational values

NEAC recognises that an individual's professional ability is more than the sum of his or her competences and will include already-acquired knowledge and essential attributes such as integrity, humour and intelligence. However, experience has proved that looking at performance in terms of competences provides valuable insights and suggests strategies for development which are both simple and achievable.

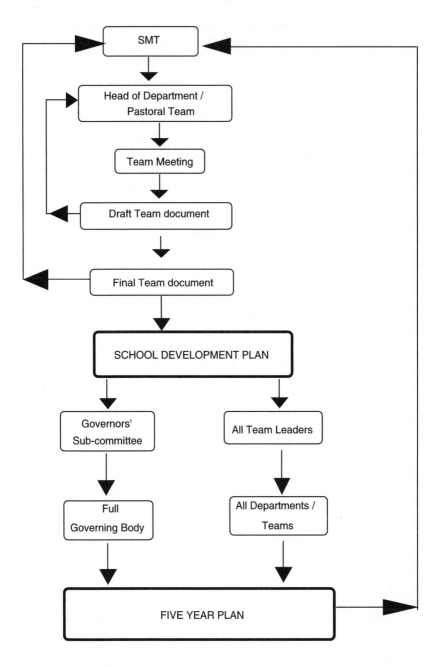

Figure 10.5 Team development in relation to the school development plan
Source Blandford (1997a)

NEAC assessors have extensive experience of senior management, and the majority are practising headteachers. Their work in assessing competences allows them to use their experience to support colleagues in an effective and positive way.

The process

Programmes are held at NEAC regional centres, situated throughout the UK. The NEAC Development Programme provides the participants with an objective report focused on their competences and suggests practical ways of improving performance. To ensure that maximum benefit is derived from this approach, it is essential that

- the middle manager explains the process and shares the outcomes with the headteacher;
- the head supports the middle manager in composing and implementing the resulting action plan.

The Development Programme aims to

1 introduce the NEAC definition of competence and its use in identifying and implementing ways of improving performance;
2 give participants objective evidence about their competences;
3 provide them with a framework within which to reflect on their own performance and needs in producing their developmental action plans.

SUMMARY

This chapter has shown that since the Education Reform Act (1988) the role of middle managers in schools has developed into a function that encompasses whole-school responsibilities.

All school teams – nursery, primary, special and secondary – now have managers whose responsibilities were hitherto in the domain of sector managers or LEAs. While teachers' primary focus remains the context of learning, all members of the profession are now required to develop the skills needed for the effective management of policies, resources and people.

A middle manager is a manager of teams, managing the skills and abilities of colleagues and, as such, is required to have knowledge and understanding of whole-school issues. These will be determined by the government, the LEA, the senior management team (SMT) and the governors. An effective middle manager will be able to identify the different influences on his/her job. The structure of the school as a learning organisation will give a clear view of his/her position within the management system.

Heads of departments and curriculum leaders play an important part in the drive towards improved standards of teaching and learning, and the government (DfEE 1999) believes that schools should recognise the importance of their contribution when allocating training budgets.

The issue of middle-management training is a focus of current debate. Much can be done to train middle managers within their schools, as the next chapter's consideration of in-house training provision shows.

11

MANAGING PROFESSIONAL
DEVELOPMENT AS A RESOURCE

INTRODUCTION

Professional development includes on-the-job and in-house activities. When considering how to resource suitable training, it is important to identify areas of expertise that are available within the school as a useful source. Trainers require relevant up-to-date experience, as practitioners want to learn from those with the practical as well as the theoretical expertise.

Figure 11.1 illustrates the range of activities available to schools in the management of professional development. These fall into two approaches:

1   professional education and training
2   professional support.

This chapter considers the relationship of each approach to the practical activities that are generated within schools, thus utilising the potential to manage professional development as a resource.

Professional development co-ordinators should recognise that if individual appraisal targets and school aims are to be met important decisions about training provision and its mode of delivery have to be made. Prior to the selection of a professional development activity, the potential impact on practice of the types of training available will need to be considered. Figure 11.2 is self-explanatory, and shows that coaching, or mentoring, is likely to have a greater impact on practice than the introduction of theory. 'Doing' is the key word: wherever possible, staff should be involved in activities that relate to specified targets in order to generate the requisite quality outcomes.

The chapter considers and offers advice on professional development provision that relates to

1   induction
2   mentoring
3   self-development

4   job-exchange, job-rotation and job shadowing
5   INSET courses
6   external consultants
7   management development.

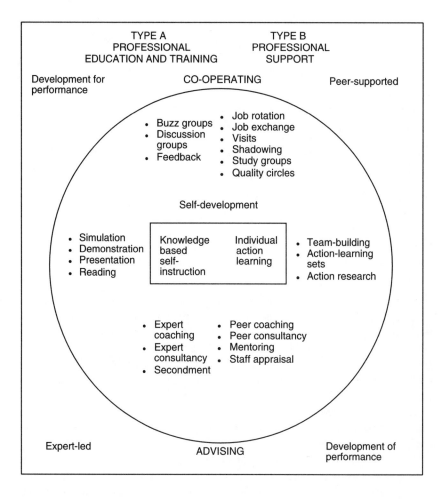

Figure 11.1   Professional development opportunities
Source Manchester LEA (1996)

INDUCTION

Teaching is an increasingly challenging career, and effective induction for newly qualified teachers or new appointments is vital if teachers are to settle quickly in their professional roles (Shaw et al. 1995). The government now

Effect	Element	Outcome
Low impact ↑	1. THEORY What and Why? 2. DEMONSTRATION How?	• Understanding of current issues • Knowledge of key concepts • Understanding of skills
	3. PRACTICE Let me try 4. FEEDBACK How did I do?	• Performance-based learning • Evaluation of outcomes
↓ High impact	5. ACTION PLAN How to use?	• Plan to improve and support • Performance in the job
	6. COACHING How am I using?	• Support for and improved performance in the job

Figure 11.2   Essential elements of skills training
Source Oldroyd and Hall (1991)

requires a year-long induction for newly qualified teachers, and considers induction to be a means of identifying failing teachers at the start of their professional lives (Statutory Instruments 1999). In any profession, the transition from training to the workplace generates uncertainties, and just as inductees need to be reassured about their progress their managers should ensure that their potential to progress is not impeded through lack of appropriate training. Effective induction should ensure that newly qualified teachers, or any teachers new to the school, feel supported and confident, ready to join an effective team, and willing to contribute to their own and the school's development.

Documentation of relevant information should be prepared by the manager, in advance of the selection interviews for a vacant post, for the new appointee to take away. The manager should then arrange times when the appointee can visit the school and the department to meet new colleagues and pupils. This visit should be carefully planned to reflect the needs of both the appointee and the school. A new appointee will require access to information relating to

- the job – a full job description is required;
- the team to which he or she is assigned – introductions to team members and their roles;

- school personnel – introductions to colleagues;
- the school's aims (SDP);
- departmental aims (DDP);
- the organisation of the school;
- reporting and assessment procedures;
- school policies;
- identities of vulnerable pupils;
- contract (including start date and timetable);
- staff handbook;
- health and safety details;
- staff lists;
- layout of school buildings, room and class lists;
- specimen reports and assessment forms;
- schemes of work and lesson plans.

The professional development co-ordinator can encourage appropriate staff members to become involved in the induction programme, actively promoting the development of newly appointed individuals. Such staff will need to be informed as to how to plan effective and flexible induction. Consideration might be given to a process with the following components:

- assigning a mentor to new appointees;
- identifying the training, development and personal needs of the new appointees;
- negotiating with new colleagues to decide the most appropriate personal and professional support;
- arrangements for job shadowing and observation to lay the foundation for reflective practice;
- ensuring that the newly appointed staff are introduced to their teams;
- ensuring that new appointees know their roles and their managers;
- consideration of external factors, such as arrangements for accommodation, transport and social needs;
- ensuring that support and professional guidance are relevant;
- planning and monitoring a central induction programme to enable newcomers to meet with staff and discuss their strengths and weaknesses; this programme may begin prior to the inductees taking up their posts;
- providing access to external support networks and groups, subject organisations and LEA advisers.

MENTORING

An important aspect of induction and staff development is mentoring – a term which is used in several different ways and contexts in education (Ormston and Shaw 1993). It generally means the positive support offered by experienced staff to staff with less experience of the school. This experience can extend over a wide range of activities, or be specific to one activity. Teachers, including middle and senior managers, may engage in a number of mentoring relationships:

- mentoring of trainee teachers;
- mentoring of registered teachers;
- mentoring of licensed teachers;
- mentoring of newly qualified teachers joining their teams;
- mentoring of colleagues to support them in their new roles.

Mentoring roles will vary, according to need, from a vocational to an interpersonal focus:

1 *Vocational: career development* Vocational mentoring roles include: enhancing the subject's skills and intellectual development; helping to develop a set of educational values; consulting to help the subject to clarify goals and ways of implementing them; helping to establish a set of personal and professional standards; and networking and sponsoring by providing opportunities for the subject to meet other professionals. These roles help newly qualified teachers, new appointments, and those new to middle management or headships to adjust to changes in their career pattern and to advance within the profession.

2 *Interpersonal: support in current role* Interpersonal mentoring roles include: sharing; role modelling; and allowing the subject to gain insight into how the mentor works in a professional capacity. A mentor should also encourage the subject to build his or her self-confidence by acknowledging successes. A mentor is also a counsellor who listens to but does not tell the subject what to do. Not all mentors will fulfil all of these roles, but the more extensive the roles, the richer the relationship. These roles enable the subject to clarify his or her identity and to develop professional confidence and self-esteem.

Those who act as mentors are likely to have a number of roles within the school and so should have some say about who to mentor in the context of their other tasks and responsibilities. Mentoring is time-consuming. Subjects should (assuming their freedom of choice) select a mentor on the basis of professional needs, present or future. It is important to understand that mentoring is a continuous staff development activity which, once a system is in place, happens during normal school life.

The essential elements of a mentoring relationship are

- a recognisable procedure, formal or informal;
- a clear understanding of the procedure and of the roles of mentor and subject;
- trust, confidentiality, discretion and a rapport between both parties;
- mentors with the requisite professional credibility and integrity and a range of suitable skills, including counselling, listening, sensitive questioning, analysis and handing back responsibilities;
- subjects who are aware of their own needs;
- attitudes appropriate to the roles of mentor and mentored: for example, professional concern on the part of the mentor to challenge the subject, and the self-motivation on the subject's part to willingly take the necessary action.

Senior management should give consideration to any issues of equality of opportunity that need to be addressed in the selection and training of mentors.

Mentoring is a positive mechanism for developing management skills, while those who have been subject to mentoring will have gained from the experience a sense of what their ongoing professional development will involve. The mentoring process should move through the stages shown in Figure 11.3.

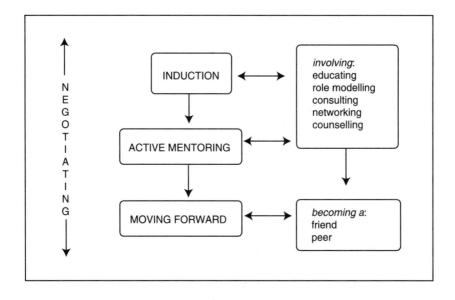

Figure 11.3   Stages of mentoring
Source Blandford (1998b)

The process will involve a period of induction for both mentor and subject which encompasses educating, role modelling, consulting, networking and counselling. During this stage, both mentor and subject should consider their compatibility in-role.

Active mentoring will involve further negotiations between mentor and subject. A framework for developing the relationship should be agreed. Changes will occur as the relationship moves gradually towards a balanced equality. Once specific targets are reached, a sense of equality is readily acknowledged. If the relationship is ordered in terms of hierarchy, there may be difficulty on both sides in recognising the true meaning of the process. At no time should a sense of rank be allowed to dominate the relationship. The mentor's interpersonal skills are essential in ensuring that rank does not intrude.

In short, mentoring is a process through which knowledge and under-standing, skills and abilities, may be passed on to less-experienced practitioners. As a method of developing teachers' professional competence, it has proven qualities (Squire and Blandford 1997). There are, however, some potential drawbacks to mentoring. For example, mentors may

- pass on bad habits;
- be unqualified or unable to impart their knowledge of their job;
- lack the patience required;
- be reluctant to pass on their skills;
- be too closely involved to see their job from another person's perspective.

The following guidance on how to create a mentor scheme may be useful:

1   Ensure that all staff and governors are fully aware of the scheme. This limits

    - animosity from teachers who are not on the mentor programme;
    - middle managers' irritation because of mentoring demands on teachers in their departments;
    - the anxiety of governors, who may see it as a system which promotes 'favourites'.

2   Nominate a trained senior member of staff to manage the scheme and to train mentors in coaching, guidance and counselling.
3   Both subjects and mentors should be volunteers, but where selectivity is necessary the qualities to be identified in the subjects are assertiveness, a positive outlook and the willingness to work hard and to learn. Mentors should be expert practitioners, who are empathetic and have the inter-personal skills to coach, encourage self-assessment, impart skills, foster innovation, argue and discuss.

4   Pair mentors with suitable subjects to maximise benefits. This may require the involvement of the departmental or year head in mentoring activities.
5   Assess the outcomes of the scheme, weighing the development of the teachers against any problems experienced. Ensure that the mentors gain in credit, experience and career prospects.

SELF DEVELOPMENT

An alternative approach to professional development is self-development. Carr and Kemmis (1986) consider that theory and knowledge are capable of transforming a teacher's beliefs and values. In the process of reflecting on one's performance, interaction with educational theory may not dictate a change of practice, but it may transform the outlook of the practitioner. Providing individuals with new concepts is a means by which to offer them not merely a new way of thinking, but the opportunity of increasing their awareness of how they function professionally. The full task of self-reflection and evaluation requires a teacher to collaborate in decisions that will transform the situation. The process of self-evaluation encompasses assessing how well one interacts with colleagues and with the school as an organisation. Teachers should consider, therefore, whether they are in a school which is right for them.

Professional development is systemic and continous. The art of self-evaluation is acquired against a background of continual learning. As Senge (1990: 142) made clear

> People with a high level of personal mastery live in a continual learning mode. They never 'arrive'. People with a high level of personal mastery are acutely aware of their ignorance, their incompetence, and their growth areas, and they are deeply self-confident. Paradoxical? Only for those who do not see that the journey is the reward.

In practice, self-development involves making sense of ourselves and our actions in situations. Key issues for consideration are one's

- relationship with self (self-evaluation)
- ability to develop
- level of empowerment – status and sense of worth
- choices and opportunities for individualistic activities

Personal qualities needed for self-development include

- the capacity for self-management

- clear personal values and objectives
- a commitment to personal growth
- a willingness to engage with problems
- creative and innovative tendencies

In practice, reflective professional development includes such characteristics as

- a concern to try to make sense of ourselves in our situations;
- a commitment to the development 'of self' by 'self';
- preference for human-agency over social-formation explanations;
- application of learning-organisation and adult-growth theories;
- individual or group self-development;
- a focus on the whole person rather than a person's competences;
- recognising that there are choices to be made – empowerment.

Self-development involves an individual's advances in learning and understanding in the context of job and career. Practitioners should have a clear view of what their own jobs are about, the relationship between teaching and management, the school development plan and so on; senior staff should also have an understanding of their position in relation to those they manage. As Isaac (1995) has commented: 'Developing yourself ... depends on the extent to which you recognise issues from your reflection, and learn to change your behaviour.'

Self-development begins with self-evaluation. A starting-point for this process could be the career aspirations of individual practitioners. Key questions to pose in self-evaluation are:

1 What do I value?
2 What is my present situation?
3 Where would I like my career to lead?
4 How might I get there?
5 What help is available?

One means of developing the skills required for self-evaluation is to consider the range of knowledge that exists regarding educational practice. This may include

- common-sense knowledge about practice that is simply assumption or opinion; for example, the view that students need discipline;
- folk-wisdom of teachers, such as the view that pupils get restless on windy days;
- skill knowledge used by teachers;

- contextual knowledge: the background knowledge about this class, this community or pupil, against which ... aspirations [are measured];
- professional knowledge about teaching strategies and the curriculum;
- educational theory: ideas about the development of individuals, or about the role of education in society;
- social and moral theories and general philosophical outlook about how people can and should interact ... uses of knowledge in society, or about truth and justice.

A practice-based approach to self-evaluation is shown in Figure 11.4. In this example, questions for teachers to ask of themselves relate to:

- *teamworking* – listening, attitude, flexibility
- *relationships* – with parents, colleagues, pupils
- *knowledge* – of current publications, equality of opportunity issues, learning styles
- *preparation* – of lessons, monitoring procedures, assessment

Self-evaluation should inform day-to-day practice. The effective teacher will be effective also in self-evaluation. He or she will regularly ask: 'Where am I in relation to these four elements of practice?'

JOB EXCHANGE AND JOB SHADOWING

An outcome of self-evaluation may be the individual's recognition of his or her need to extend understanding of a particular role. This can be achieved through job exchange or job shadowing.

Job Exchange

The practice of exchanging jobs may appear to be difficult to operate in the subject-based environment of the National Curriculum; however, as a means of developing staff, job exchange can provide high-impact training opportunities. The key is preparation and planning.

To begin with, information should be compiled on individual learning needs and favoured learning styles. Teachers undergoing job exchange should consider where learning and development opportunities exist in school, set realistic targets for learning and development, plan appropriate activities and review achievement (and, if necessary, the reasons for any shortfall). Decisions should then be taken, if additional learning is required, as to whether self-directed study or consultation over progress with a manager is necessary.

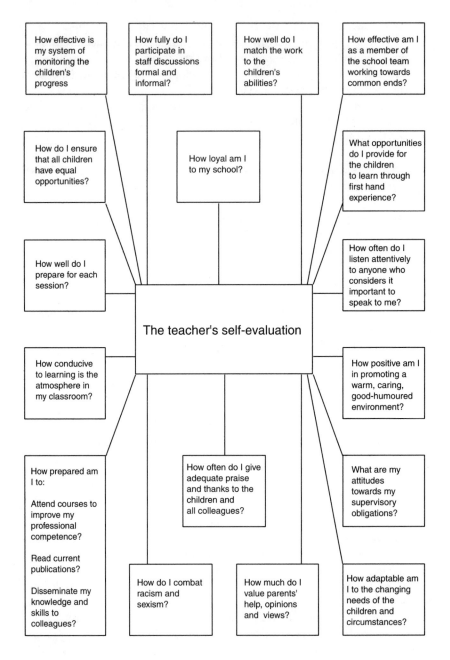

Figure 11.4   A model of self-evaluation for teachers
Source Manchester LEA (1986)

Job Shadowing

Job shadowing and classroom observation might appear to be merely different descriptions of a single activity. There are, however, distinctions to be made between the two: job shadowing has a longer duration; its aim is to learn by watching someone at work rather than to collect feedback on specific aspects of a teacher's performance; it is also more open ended in intention. Indeed, it may be used to identify aspects of performance for specific observation.

A job-shadowing exercise may have a learning objective which is so specific as to require only a half-day's shadowing; the more general the learning objective, the more protracted the duration. It is perhaps as close as you can get to experiencing someone's job from his or her point of view. It can also give a taste of the realities of the work, with all its unexpected interruptions and events. As such, job shadowing may be used to address learning requirements that range from the highly specific to the general and holistic. However, care needs to be taken to ensure that both shadower and shadowed are clear on what they expect from it. Figure 11.5 provides a template for the analysis of practice when job shadowing.

Date: Lesson: Lesson Plan: Include all details	
Targets:	Record Time Taken
Comment/Analysis:	
Action Points:	

Figure 11.5   Prompt sheet

MANAGEMENT DEVELOPMENT

Job exchanges and other self-directed projects will be effective only with the support of middle and senior managers. Senior staff can help to encourage in-school training by engendering an environment conducive to on-site learning, and by organising in-house learning opportunities.

Managers themselves have developmental requirements. Their development should be viewed as a means of increasing the general management capability of the school's leadership. There are numerous management development activities available (Wallace 1986), including

- action-centred leadership
- action learning
- assertiveness training
- award-bearing courses
- brainstorming techniques
- learning from case studies
- coaching and counselling skills
- developing consultancy skills
- critical friendship
- development training
- job analysis
- job enrichment
- job rotation
- learning contracts
- management review
- networking
- peer-assisted leadership
- performance appraisal

Participation in management development is possible in a number of modes:

- distance learning
- external training programmes
- private study
- quality circles
- school exchanges
- self development
- short courses

INSET

The collective approach to professional development is whole-school INSET. The General Teaching Council's list of the criteria for effective INSET begins with the recognition by teachers of their training needs as they relate to the objectives of the school, the LEA and the government, as supported by the headteacher and other staff (GTC 1993). Coherent school and LEA policies will provide the basis for the precise targeting of provision and the selection of appropriate forms of INSET, whether school-based or external. Furthermore, in order to have an impact on classroom practice, all INSET should have a practical focus, with appropriate post-training follow-up in the school.

Research has shown that effective INSET can take diverse forms and have a number of key characteristics (NFER 1990), including the clear identification of aims and objectives and an analysis of training needs to ensure development activities match existing levels of expertise and the aims of the school. The NFER found that opportunities for reflection are important, as is action research, ongoing evaluation and follow-up work. Effective use of existing school resources and facilities depends upon in-service activities being well planned. This will promote targeted and tailor-made INSET, as well as minimising disruption. The introduction of school development plans has encouraged more effective planning, and the role of the INSET (professional development) co-ordinator is central to this process, at both the school and the LEA level. Figure 11.6 illustrates the relationship between INSET and outcomes.

EFFECTIVENESS OF INSET	MAIN FOCUS	ACTIVITIES
AS RITUAL	Emphasis on delivery throughout Taking part ... Using up the budget	• ANYTHING GOES!
FOR KNOWING	Emphasis on awareness-raising Knowing about ...	• PRESENTATION OF THEORY AND DESCRIPTION
FOR DOING	Emphasis on skills development Knowing how ...	• DEMONSTRATION • PRACTICE • FEEDBACK
FOR USING	Emphasis on action planning and transfer of learning into unique social setting Planning how ...	• PLANNING • COACHING • FEEDBACK

Figure 11.6 INSET's several functions in terms of focus and activities

Source Oldroyd and Hall (1991)

In ensuring effective INSET provision the issues to be considered are several, and may be summarised as follows:

1 Training needs are identified at school level following appraisals or the drawing up of the school development plan.
2 The teachers whose needs have been identified are those selected for training. There are no substitutions.
3 Heads and senior managers are fully aware of the purpose of the training and the expected outcomes.
4 The training forms part of a coherent programme and is not a 'one-off'.
5 The training requires preparatory work by the participating teachers, and may be sufficiently extensive to require further work, reflection and consolidation in school between sessions.
6 The trainers are fully briefed.
7 Training groups are comparatively homogeneous or the training is targeted to the identified needs of the participants and sufficiently differentiated to take account of their varying levels of expertise.
8 The range of provision can include on- and off-site courses, guided reading, classroom support, local support groups and distance-learning materials.
9 Dissemination strategies are built into the course. Participants are given the time to disseminate what they have learnt and are encouraged to do so.
10 Training is followed by some form of support in school.

Planning for INSET, depending on its type and purpose, may require several months of review and consultation (see Chapter 8), and staff should not be expected to accommodate suggestions immediately. Professional development programmes should be planned by a team representing the interests of all staff levels as indicated in Figure 11.7. Once planned, the programme should be circulated and views sought from colleagues on approaches appropriate to each element. The final details should reflect staff needs and concerns, which themselves should relate directly to pupil needs.

It is essential that teachers are trained at a suitably professional level. The style, content and relevance of INSET provision will need to be complemented by appropriate management. Consideration of adult learning styles (see Chapter 1 and The Appendix) illuminates the importance of recognising which teaching and learning styles are appropriate in the training programmes (Honey and Mumford 1982). A headteacher who considers that a 'stand and deliver' approach to training will encourage staff participation might be considered naive. In order for staff to feel confident that their involvement will be respected and valued the approach should be supportive. They should be given the opportunity to reflect, individually and in groups, on the material presented during training.

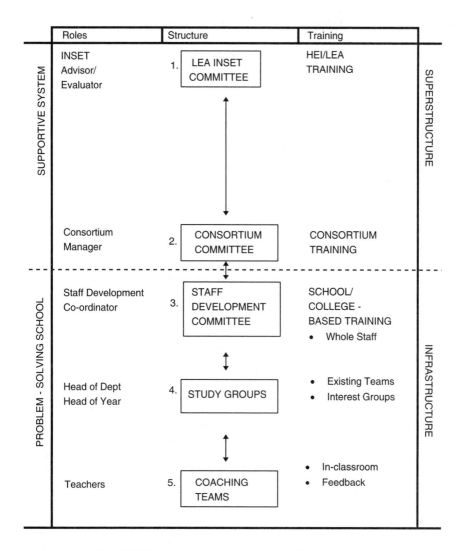

Roles	Structure	Training

SUPPORTIVE SYSTEM / **SUPERSTRUCTURE**

INSET Advisor/ Evaluator — 1. LEA INSET COMMITTEE — HEI/LEA TRAINING

Consortium Manager — 2. CONSORTIUM COMMITTEE — CONSORTIUM TRAINING

PROBLEM - SOLVING SCHOOL / **INFRASTRUCTURE**

Staff Development Co-ordinator — 3. STAFF DEVELOPMENT COMMITTEE — SCHOOL/ COLLEGE - BASED TRAINING
• Whole Staff

Head of Dept Head of Year — 4. STUDY GROUPS — • Existing Teams • Interest Groups

Teachers — 5. COACHING TEAMS — • In-classroom • Feedback

Figure 11.7   LEA–INSET structure for continuing professional development
Source Oldroyd and Hall (1991)

Appropriate information should be circulated in advance to enable staff to consider their position in relation to important policies, procedures and practices. The presentation should be varied and designed to stimulate interest: a mass of printed sheets will generate little response from staff with busy professional lives. Information should be relevant and accessible, and presented in a succinct style. Long lists and complex prose will not be appreciated. It is important that staff should engage with the key issues in an informed way, and that they understand the essentials relating to their practice.

INSET should focus on issues that are relevant to the individual school and which will lead to a confirmation or a change of practice. If staff are to derive full value from the training, they will need to feel confident that they are working with colleagues they trust and who will allow them to be open. INSET co-ordinators should plan the composition of groups with care, not allowing dominant individuals to take over and intimidate others. All staff should be committed to an honest approach to discussion of individual and whole-school problems. The use of case studies will enable staff to share concerns about a particular problem. All discussions should be solution-orientated, emphasising the 'can-do' approach to development that celebrates and praises good practice.

The frequency of INSET days, half-days or twilight sessions may impact on the quality of participation in the programme and its outcomes. Isolated days that are scheduled randomly throughout the year will not promote inclusive and active debate on policy, procedure and practice. Time needs to be invested in building a positive and supportive atmosphere for staff. Given the restrictions of the school day, whole days of training followed by twilight sessions might provide the most appropriate structure, and senior managers and teams would have to consider this aspect of organisation in their planning.

The venue, too, is important. It is sometimes beneficial to have an off-site venue to generate the right atmosphere for teachers to feel confident. When INSET is school-based, the careful selection of rooms, chairs, tables and display equipment is important. The room should be large enough to accommodate the group in comfort, without being too large. Chairs should be comfortable, uniform in style, but not arranged in rows. Tables should be provided if staff are expected to write. Display equipment (video, overhead projector and flip-charts) should be clearly visible to all. Technical equipment should be checked before the session. If staff are required to write, pens, pencils and paper should be available.

In short, the requirements for effective INSET programmes are:

- detailed planning and a close match to identified need;
- clear objectives which are agreed with participants;
- provision which has a clear relationship to classroom needs;
- use of teachers' prior knowledge and experiences;
- adequate provision of follow-up activity;
- a mutually supportive but self-critical disposition among participants who are committed to the raising of standards;
- support and encouragement of senior managers with realistic expectations.

Subject-Based INSET

A team approach to INSET may focus on subject-based issues. In the great majority of schools, and in most curricular areas, teachers have sufficient command of the subjects they teach and adequate pedagogic skills to deliver them satisfactorily to the groups assigned. However, in a substantial minority of schools there are teachers whose command of their subject is weak or where there are inadequacies in key aspects of methodology, such as the use of inappropriate activities, and ill-paced and unchallenging lessons. Local circumstances and national shortages mean that some schools are unable to provide specialist teaching for all their pupils, so that some teachers are obliged to teach lessons in subjects for which they lack the requisite knowledge, qualifications or experience. Additionally, many teachers are ill-equipped to teach basic literacy skills to pupils who have fallen behind their peers.

In all subjects, the expertise required of teachers is continuously evolving; in some, maintaining the requisite level of skill demands opportunities for practice beyond the teaching situation. Changes in curriculum content also need to be understood and applied. Rapid technological advances, particularly in IT, likewise demands that teachers keep abreast of their potential to contribute to the teaching of their subject. For all these reasons, regular and systematic subject-specific developmental opportunities through in-service training, both for specialists and non-specialists, remains a major concern if schools are to maintain and improve their effectiveness.

The positive effects of subject-based INSET include:

- a more confident grasp of subject knowledge;
- a heightened awareness of different teaching methods;
- a sharper approach to meeting pupils' needs;
- increased effectiveness of questioning techniques;
- improvements in curriculum documentation;
- closer collaboration between SEN support staff and classroom teachers.

USING A CONSULTANT

Use of external consultants has proved expensive, in time and funding, for some schools. In selecting a consultant, managers are advised to follow some such checklist as the following, to ensure relevant outcomes and guard against unnecessary expenditure.

To begin with, schools should examine the reasons for employing an external consultant. Under such conditions as the following, it will be necessary to select and manage a consultant:

- when the specialised expertise of the consultant is not already available in the school or LEA;
- when those within the school who have the expertise to train others are already stretched by other work;
- when otherwise unavailable support is needed in the planning or delivery of an in-school training programme;
- when breadth of experience is required in assessing the potential outcomes of a proposed programme by comparison with others;
- when the school is already committed to a consultant-led programme of which the training forms a part.

In selecting a consultant, consideration should be given to a range of questions:

1   Is the consultant reliable? Check on the consultant's previous clients and discuss what was achieved; ask to see internal feedback on effectiveness of provision.
2   What is the problem? The school's management, as the client, must be clear on what exactly it is that the consultant is being asked to do. Expect the consultant to press this point until it is absolutely clear, maybe helping to redefine the problem or to uncover any hidden agendas.
3   What results are expected? The consultant will be as anxious as the client to have a desired goal or target. Write up a brief form of job description or contract in which the task is agreed.
4   Is the consultant equipped to resolve the problem?

Having selected the consultant, and agreed terms, objectives and indicators, the consultant must now be managed. Do not allow the consultant to manage the client. Work with the consultant, meet frequently, facilitate, make arrangements, make people available, and learn from the way in which the consultant operates.

Give feedback on progress at stages throughout the consultancy and again at the end. Feedback can help the quality of the consultant's performance, just as it can with that of any other employee. If there is to be a final report, discuss it with the consultant before it is finally presented; if the client has stayed in close enough contact, it should contain no surprises.

Expect follow-through activities. Beware of consultants who produce recommendations but cannot help to implement them. Consultants should be willing to face any technical or political difficulties of implementation, or else should train staff in the new skills needed. Expect also a return visit from the consultant to discuss the outcomes of the consultancy. Thereafter, it becomes a process of collaboration to ensure that the outcomes prove worthwhile to all participants.

SUMMARY

This chapter has described a range of training and development opportunities available to teachers in schools. By focusing on the management of professional development as a resource the emphasis is placed on schools as learning organisations.

Possibilities for staff development have been described within the context of school development, including: induction, mentoring, self-development, INSET courses, job exchange, management courses and the use of consultants.

Given the government's introduction of teacher-training schemes, school management teams will have responsibility for determining which of the many other professional development opportunities available to teachers should be funded.

Chapter 12 revisits many of the issues raised in this book, and concludes with a brief treatment of performance management.

12

THE WAY FORWARD

Performance management in schools

INTRODUCTION

This chapter is in two parts: a summary and commentary on the key elements of the book is presented prior to embarking on a view of the future.

This book has encompassed three key elements relating to the management of professional development in schools: management theory (TQM and the process for IIP recognition); government legislation; and planning and management. The book has attempted to show that the challenge for management teams, professional development co-ordinators and teachers is how these elements are best combined to guide and support the careers of teachers and meet the needs of the schools in which those careers unfold.

The management of the professional development of teachers is central to the government's drive to raise standards in schools. The professional development of teachers is intrinsic to institutional development. Strategic, operational and development planning and target setting are recognised as key activities for practitioners and managers in schools. The role of a professional development co-ordinator is central to the planning and implementation of professional development in order to negotiate successfully the relationship between individual and institutional needs.

Part I provided the theoretical underpinning for professional development, focusing on human resource management and total quality management (TQM). TQM is concerned with the principles of culture, communication and commitment, three powerful influences in the management of a developing school. A school's culture (its ethos), although intangible, is a constant reminder of the purpose of the institution as a learning organisation. The capacity of managers to value their staff is reflected in the culture. The freedom of individuals to communicate their concerns and their need for the support of colleagues is also an indication of a culture that embraces professional development. Handy (1993) provides models of organisational cultures that indicate how members of organisations communicate: by order, as teams, according to task, or as individuals. In

196

most cases, schools encompass elements of each of Handy's descriptions of differing organisational cultures. In practice, it is a sharing of beliefs and values and visions that provides the harmony whereby dissonance and resonance can be appreciated in equal measure as part of the everyday existence of the complex organisation that is the modern school. The importance of professional development in supporting teachers' practice is evident in this context.

Part II examined the impact of government policy on continuing professional development of teachers. Successive governments in recent times have embraced the drive to improve the standards of both teaching and learning in our schools. The present administration is continuing to underscore the importance of professional development for teachers. For five years, the Teacher Training Agency (heavily resourced by the Department for Education and Employment) has tackled the professional development of teachers from the training stage right through to refining the skills of headteachers. The TTA has developed the *National Standards for Teachers* (1998e) which embraces qualified teachers, subject leaders, special educational needs co-ordinators, and headteachers. Initial teacher education is now competence-based for primary specialists, with clear targets in English, Science, Mathematics and Information Communication Technology, and subject-based for secondary specialists in English, Mathematics and ICT. Training institutions are assessed for their ability to instruct trainees, and their funding is dependent on annual outcomes. The input–output model of training underpins ITE. Yet, practitioners and trainers have acknowledged the weaknesses in this approach to the training of teachers (Wilkin, 1998).

Following training, newly qualified teachers are to be inducted into the profession, with schools addressing the targets set by training institutions and specified in the NQTs' career entry profiles. Each profile forms the basis of a practitioner's assessment of his or her teaching skills. For the teacher with developed skills, there is the potential of either fast-tracking to headship or moving beyond the performance threshold to Advanced Skills Teacher status.

An alternative for teachers aspiring to management is to pursue the National Professional Qualification for Subject Leaders, currently in the early stages of development. Meanwhile, LEAs, teachers' unions, HEIs, NEAC centres and the *Times Educational Supplement* (DoE 1999) have identified training for middle management as an area requiring development; at present the attempt to meet this need is through short-course provision.

Having embarked upon the continuum of professional development, successful teachers and managers have opportunities for further training at their chosen level or they may opt to be trained for headship. The National Professional Qualification for Headship (NPQH) is a practice-based programme that provides training for aspirant and serving headteachers. The impact of this programme in raising schools' standards is yet to be determined. The first candidates to complete the NPQH have acknowledged the value of the training. However, the TTA (see Green 1999) has expressed doubts over the equating of NPQH accreditation with suitability for headship. The TTA has recently recognised the importance of *emotional intelligence*, not previously mentioned in its literature. Further research is needed into the crucial relationship of interpersonal skills to the attributes required by the national standards in preparation for school leadership.

The Headteacher Leadership and Management Programme for newly appointed headteachers has had more of a mixed reception from participants than has the NPQH. The idea that the £2,500 with which each new head-teacher may purchase training from registered HEADLAMP providers is available for two years from the time of appointment has not met with uniform enthusiasm from the profession. Newly appointed headteachers believe that they require more time in post prior to the selection of courses (Squire and Blandford 1997). Participants were also found to have had varied experiences in terms of the quality of provision of induction, needs analysis, training and development.

A course is now available for serving headteachers. In partnership with Hay McBer, the TTA has developed a programme that will enable serving headteachers to reflect on their practice within the framework of the national standards. Again, the effectiveness of this programme has yet to be evaluated in terms of its impact on standards, though to date participants are reported to be very positive about their experiences.

The government's investment in the professional development of teachers is to be welcomed. There are, however, questionable facets to certain operational and policy decisions. The TTA has at times distanced itself from educators by seeking the advice of agents outside the education sector, particularly in respect of management development. There would appear to be a paradox here, in that the emphasis is on raising classroom (pedagogic) standards while the leadership training is in the corporate mode, as provided by business. Is there a need to return to leadership with a distinctively educational perspective? While many educators (e.g. Bush et al. 1999) recognise the need to share expertise and would welcome such an approach to the professional development of school leaders, the government has yet to recognise its value.

Part III has focused on the practical implications of managing professional development in schools. Planning is a prerequisite of any management or educational activity. The importance of the school development plan in relation to professional development has been a central theme of this book. Both school and individual targets are achievable within the context of a detailed plan that identifies SMART objectives and relates them to available resources. As Chapter 8 argued, the appraisal process is the mechanism that links individual with school targets. In practice, appraisal is the developmental tool by which individuals may analyse strengths and weaknesses in order to raise their standards of performance as teachers and managers in schools. If professional development is to be the means of raising standards in schools, further investment is required in needs analysis and the provision of training and development opportunities.

Middle management, as was said above, is an area of professional development in schools in need of training, development and resources. As player–managers, subject and year co-ordinators have a significant role to play in boosting individual, team and whole-school performance. Yet promotion to a management position has tended to be based on classroom rather than managerial skills. Knowledge and understanding of teams and management roles are crucial to effective middle management of schools, and further investment in the analysis of the role, and training are therefore required.

Having appraised teachers and managers in order to inform and respond to the plans that develop the school, the next task is to put into operation that which has been agreed: the raising of standards through the achievement of targets. As has been argued throughout this book, the management of professional development as a resource is fundamental to a learning organisation. The government (DfEE 1998b) has commented on the importance of professional learning to the fulfilment of a school's vision. In addition, there is an emphasis in current thinking on lifelong learning (see Thompson 1999) on developing the capabilities of individuals. It should be recognised that lifelong learning encompasses the development of cognitive capacities alongside the development of skills. The government proposes (DfEE 1998b) that, through the management of learning accounts, teachers will have opportunities to register for higher degrees in education at Master and Doctoral levels. Importantly, the professional Doctorate in Education (EdD) is predicated, unusually for research at this level, on the relationship between theory and practice in education.

There are many opportunities for the professional development of teachers, including induction, job shadowing, mentoring and INSET. If managed effectively, school-based development will achieve positive outcomes for all, – teachers, pupils and schools – as evidenced by the raising of standards through effective learning.

THE FUTURE: PERFORMANCE MANAGEMENT

Performance management, which is central to the government's proposals for the appraisal and professional development of teachers, is a means of expressing the relationship between appraisal, individual and whole-school development planning, target-setting and progress monitoring. There is a difficulty here, however, in that the government's intention (DfEE 1999) is to relate performance management to pay. If pay were removed from the equation, performance management would provide a useful and effective summation of the key themes discussed in this book: TQM, career development, planning, developmental appraisal and school-based training and development.

In the world of business, performance management is a strategic approach designed to deliver sustained success (see Thompson, 1999) through its focus on productivity. The DfEE (1998b) claims that

> systematic performance management is key to achievement in organisations. In schools, it motivates teachers to give of their best and provides school managers with the tools to deploy and develop their staff most efficiently. It should encompass a robust system for appraising staff against clear objectives and outcomes, and ensure that proper links exist between performance, pay, career progression and professional development.

In brief, performance management is an integrated strategy concerned with improvement and development of organisational productivity. It relates to TQM, in part, through its emphasis on inputs, outputs and communication. Another similarity with TQM is its willingness to retain older elements alongside new ideas. Investors In People similarly embraces the relationship of the old to the new in the systems and structures that allow for growth and creativity.

For the individual, performance management is a sophisticated process that focuses on the following:

- the personal
- leadership
- teams
- systems
- the contextual

As with TQM, the importance of culture here is manifest. However, the issue of performance-related pay and its impact on appraisal is having a detrimental affect on teachers' views of performance management. The government considers that the new pay and performance management arrangements are designed to improve the performance of schools by:

- attracting, motivating and retaining high quality teachers;
- raising standards of pupil attainment by establishing clear connections between pupil performance and teachers' objectives;
- linking increased rewards to good performance, and permitting the best teachers to progress faster;

- ensuring for all teachers better opportunities for career and professional development relating to school targets and their own career aspirations.

The Institute of Personnel Development has advised teaching unions' representatives (Thompson 1999) that performance-related pay enhances strategic objectives. In the drive to add value to the profession, the government has also recognised changes in employees' expectations. The Green Paper (DfEE 1998b) has anticipated such demands with the introduction of learning accounts and professional development contracts. These proposals also meet OfSTED's criticism (OfSTED News 9 1999), that the appraisal system lacks rigour and has rarely been followed through.

The adoption of performance management is inevitable and has implications for school managers, who will become performance analysts further developing their knowledge of

- the organisation (structures and systems)
- available data (appraisal, leagues tables)
- the culture (people, formal and social ethos)
- individuals (functions, performance targets)
- professional and psychological needs of colleagues (career development, beliefs and personal histories)

Managers will also be performance strategists, in their functions as

- leaders
- entrepreneurs
- innovators
- networkers

In essence, managers will be 'big-picture' thinkers, responsible for performance enhancement, which leads to a set of complex issues. Performance enhancement links to the coaching function (Mumford 1997), whereby the manager is a motivator, mentor and *helper*.

As Green (1999) made clear, in a comment cited earlier in this chapter, the significance of emotional intelligence in this context is considerable. Stoll and Fink (1998) have researched the relationship between culture and performance management, and have analysed schools' internal capacity for change. Again, this is an area that resonates with TQM, HRM and development issues: people management is the key. Trust and job satisfaction, as reflected in organisational culture emanating from the personal integrity of managers, will be among the professional expectations of teachers. Professional development can enhance practitioners' receptivity to performance management through their understanding of the culture of the learning organisation.

The government proposes that in practice the performance management arrangements will comprise of two main elements:

1   Each teacher will be appraised annually by his or her senior manager on the basis of agreed objectives. The teacher's needs for continuing professional development will also be assessed.
2   At the second stage of the review, the assessment of the teacher's performance will be used by the head as the basis for a recommendation which will, in turn, inform the governing body's decision about that teacher's pay for the coming year.

In order to implement the new appraisal procedures, each school's governing body will be required to ensure that a new performance management policy is in place, setting out how the school will implement the statutory provisions for appraisal and pay. The government proposes (DfEE1998b) that policies will need to cover:

• how effective performance management will be used to improve the performance of teachers, so raising pupil attainment;
• the arrangements for carrying out appraisal at the school: timetable, responsibilities, and who has access to the assessments of teachers' performance;
• the school's arrangements for training and development, including training in the performance management system;
• arrangements for internal monitoring and evaluation.

The government also proposes that there will be an external assessor responsible for reviewing the school's overall policy on performance management. For threshold assessments, the assessor will review the paperwork documenting the head's recommendations, discussing these with the head, determining whether national standards have been met, conducting interviews or classroom observations in a sample of cases and validating recommendations. The DfEE (1998b) recommends that the management of training will encompass the following:

1   Training needs are identified at school level following appraisal or the drawing up of the school development plan.
2   The teachers whose needs are identified are selected for training. There are no substitutions. More than one teacher from each school attends.
3   Heads and senior managers are fully aware of the purpose of the training and the expected outcome.
4   The training forms part of a coherent programme, and is not a 'one-off'.

5   The training requires preparatory work by the teachers, and is suffi-
    ciently extensive to allow work in school before and between sessions, so
    enabling reflection and consolidation.
6   Trainers are fully briefed.
7   Training groups are comparatively homogeneous, or else the training is
    targeted to the identified needs of the participants and sufficiently
    differentiated to take account of their varying levels of expertise.
8   The range of provision includes on- and off-site courses, guided reading,
    classroom support, support groups and distance-learning materials.
9   Dissemination strategies are built into the course. Participants are given
    the time to disseminate what they have learned, and are encouraged to
    do so.
10 Training is followed by some form of support in school.

The implementation of best practice, as indicated by theorists, the government and practitioners, is the challenge to be addressed by the profession.
As Mumford (1997) has said, the transition from school to learning organisation – a transition which embraces performance management – is possible
only when

•   learning is central to the management process, not adopted as an
    external activity;
•   the processes and procedures that encourage learning within the organi-
    sation are led by managers;
•   learning is recognised as a continuous process;
•   learning is driven by a shared concern for improvement.

The importance of culture in this context cannot be overstated. Teachers (as
both learners and professionals) will develop in a secure, if challenging, environment. Professional development will not be effective if support and
guidance are imposed. As schools move forward, the standard of teachers'
performance is essential to their success and so must be maintained. The
management of teachers' professional development is of central importance
to schools' capacity to meet the challenge of change.
    Good luck.

APPENDIX
LEARNING STYLES QUESTIONNAIRE

The questionnaire set out below is based on Honey and Mumford's analysis (1982) of the learning cycle.

Stages of learning cycle/Learning style

Experiencing   Activist: 'I'll try anything once'
Reflecting   Reflector: 'I'd like time to think about this'
Theorising   Theorist: 'How does this fit with that?'
Testing   Pragmatist: 'How can I apply this in practice?'

Honest answers, given spontaneously, allow you to see which of the four is your predominant style or the style towards which you instinctively incline. This is a way of helping you to identify your own learning style. Please complete the questionnaire by ticking the statements with which you agree, and then to identify your learning style compare the numbers of the questions ticked with those listed in the score sheet at the end of the questionnaire.

1   I take risks if I feel justified in doing so.
2   I tend to approach problems by using a step-by-step approach to find solutions, taking care to avoid any fanciful ideas.
3   I have a no-nonsense direct style.
4   I have often found that actions prompted by feelings are as appropriate as those based on careful thought and analysis.
5   The key factor in judging a proposed idea or solution is knowing, through experience whether it works in practice.
6   When I hear about a new idea or approach I tend to start working out how to apply it in practice as soon as possible.
7   I like to follow a self-disciplined approach, establishing clear routines and logical thinking patterns.
8   I take pride in doing a methodically thorough job.
9   I get on better with people who are logical and analytical in their approach than with people who are given to spontaneous decisions.

10 I take care over the interpretation of the data available to me, and avoid jumping to conclusions.

11 I like to reach a decision carefully after weighing up the alternatives.

12 I'm attracted more to new and unusual ideas than to practical ones.

13 I dislike situations that I cannot fit into a coherent pattern.

14 I like to relate my actions to general principles.

15 In meetings I have a reputation for getting straight to the point, no matter what others feel.

16 I favour having as many sources of information as possible – the more plentiful the data the better.

17 People who make flippant responses to serious issues usually irritate me.

18 I prefer to respond to events in a spontaneous and flexible manner rather than plan things out in advance.

19 I dislike having to present my conclusions under the pressure of tight deadlines.

20 I tend to judge other people's ideas in terms, principally, of their practicability.

21 I often get irritated by people who want to rush headlong into things.

22 Thinking about the present is much more important than thinking about the past or future.

23 I think that decisions based on a thorough analysis of all the relevant information are sounder than those based on intuition.

24 In meetings I enjoy contributing ideas just as they occur to me.

25 On balance, I talk more than I should, and ought to develop my listening skills.

26 In meetings I get very impatient with people who lose sight of the key objectives.

27 I enjoy communicating my ideas and opinions to others.

28 In meetings people should keep to the point and avoid indulging in fancy ideas and speculations.

29 I like to ponder many alternatives before making up my mind.

30 Considering the way they react in meetings, I reckon that I am, on the whole, more objective and less emotional in my responses than are my colleagues.

31 I am more likely to keep in the background than to take the lead by doing the talking in meetings.

32 On balance I prefer to do the listening rather than the talking.

33 Most of the time I believe that the end justifies the means.

34 Reaching the group's objectives and targets takes precedence over individual feelings and objections.

35 I do whatever seems to me necessary to get the job done.

36 I quickly get bored with detailed work requiring a methodical approach.

37 I am keen on exploring the basic assumptions, principles and theories underpinning ideas and events.

38 I like a meeting to run according to the agenda prescribed.
39 I steer clear of subjective or ambivalent discussions.
40 I enjoy the drama and excitement of a crisis.

LEARNING STYLES QUESTIONNAIRE: SCORE SHEET

Total your number of activist scores, i.e. ticks, for questions:
1, 4, 12, 18, 22, 24, 25, 27, 36, 40 =
Total your number of reflector scores, i.e. ticks, for questions:
8, 10, 11, 16, 19, 21, 23, 29, 31, 32 =
Total your number of theorist scores, i.e. ticks, for questions:
2, 7, 9, 13, 14, 17, 30, 37, 38, 39 =
Total your number of pragmatist scores, i.e. ticks, for questions:
3, 5, 6, 15, 20, 26, 28, 33, 34, 35 =

BIBLIOGRAPHY

Adams, M. (1996) 'Investors in People: the Challenge for Staff Development', *Journal of the National Association for Staff Development*, 27 June: 12–17.

Adelman, G. Jenkins, D. Kemmis, S. (1984) 'Rethinking Case Studies' in J. Bell, T. Bush, A. Fox, J. Goodley and S. Goulding (eds) *Conducting Small-Scale Investigations in Educational Management*, London: Paul Chapman.

Adey, K. and Jones, J. (1997) 'The Professional Development Coordinator', *Educational Management and Administration* 25(2):133–44.

Advisory Conciliation and Arbitration Service (ACAS) (1986) *Teachers' Dispute: Report of the Appraisal Training and Working Group*, London: ACAS.

Alberga, T. (1997) 'Time for a Check-Up', *People Management* 13 (6 February).

Anderson, A., Barker, D. and Critten, P. (1996) *Effective Self-Development: A Skills and Ability-Based Approach*, Oxford: Blackwell.

Atkinson, P. (1991) *Creating Cultural Change – the Key to Successful Total Quality Management*, London: IFS Ltd.

Baker, L. (1992) 'Preparation, Induction and Support for Newly Appointed' Headteachers and Deputy Heads, *Education Management Information Exchange*, Slough: NFER.

—— (1996) 'The Professional Development of Headteachers', *Education Management Information Exchange*, Slough: NFER.

Baker, M. (1998) 'Invasion of the Superteachers', *Times Educational Supplement*, 30 October.

—— Evans, A. and Johnston, M. (1985) *An Evaluation of the National Scheme of School Teacher Appraisal*, London: HMSO.

Barker, J. (1993) 'Towards Total Quality Management: A National Priority (reserve) Fund Project'. Darwin, Northern Territory University; in Quong, T. and Walker, A (1996) 'TQM and School Restructuring: A Case Study', *School Organisation* 16(2): 219–31.

Barrett, E., Barton, L., Furlong, J., Galvin, C., Miles, S. and Whitty, G. (1992) *Initial Teacher Education in England and Wales: A Topography*, London: Goldsmith College, University of London.

Beer, M., Spector, B., Lawrence, P., Quinn Mills, D. and Walton, R. (1985) *Human Resource Management – A General Manager's Perspective*, Chicago, IL: Free Press.

Bell, J. (1993 [1987]) *Doing Your Research Project*, Milton Keynes: Open University Press.

Bennis, W. (1959) 'Leadership Theory, Administrative Behaviour: the Problem of Authority', *Leadership Conference* 22–3 April, University of Pittsburgh: Administrative Science Centre.

—— and Nanus, B. (1985) *Leaders: the Strategies for Taking Charge*, New York: Harper & Row.

—— Belenky, A.H. and Soder, D.A. (1993) *An Effective Management Tool*, New York: Bureau of National Affairs.

Berry, T.H. (1991) *Managing the Total Quality Transformation*, New York: McGraw-Hill.

Bines, H. and Welton, J. (1995) 'Managing Partnership' in *Teacher Training and Development*, (ed.) Bines, H. and Welton, J., London: Routledge.

Blandford, S. (1995) 'The Relationship between Educational Theory, Research and Practice: A Teacher's Perspective', unpublished EdD thesis, Bristol: University of Bristol.

—— (1997a) *Middle Mangement in Schools – How to Harmonise Managing and Teaching for an Effective School*, London: Pitman.

—— (1997b) *Resource Management in Schools: Effective and Practical Strategies for the Self-Managing School*, London: Pitman.

—— (1998a) *Managing Discipline in Schools*, London: Routledge.

—— (1998b) *Professional Development Manual*, London: Financial Times Management.

—— and Squire, L. (2000) An Evaluation of the Teacher Training AgencyHeadteacher Leadership and Management Programme (HEADLAMP), *Education Management and Administration Journal* 27(4).

Blankstein, A. M. and Swain, H. (1994) 'Is TQM Right for Schools?', *Executive Educator* 16(2): 51–4.

Blunkett, D. (1999) 'I Want to Reward Performance', *The Teacher*, April.

Blyton, P. and Turnbull, P. (eds) (1992) *Reassessing Human Resource Management*, London: Sage.

Bolam, R. (1993) *Recent Developments and Emerging Issues in the Continuing Professional Development of Teachers*, London: General Teaching Council for England and Wales (GTC).

—— (1999) 'Educational Leadership, Administration and Management', paper presented at the *ESRC Seminar*, 6–7 May, West Hill House, Birmingham

—— McMahon, A., Pocklington, K. and Weindling, D. (1993) *National Evaluation of the Headteacher Mentoring Pilot Schemes: A Report for the Department for Education*, London: HMSO.

Bollington, R. and Bradley, H. (1990) *Training for Appraisal*, Cambridge: Cambridge Institute of Education.

Borg, W. R. (1981) *Applying Educational Research: A Practical Guide for Teachers*, New York: Longman.

Bostingl, J. (1993) 'The Quality Movement: What it's Really About', *Educational Leadership* 51: 66.

Brighouse, T. (1978) *Starting Point of Self-Evaluation*, Oxford: Oxfordshire Local Education Department.

Brown, M. and Rutherford, D. (1996) 'Heads of Department – Secondary Schools', paper presented at the British Education Management and Administration Society (BEMAS) *Partners in Change Conference*, 22–7 March, Cambridge.

—— and Taylor, J. (1996) 'Achieving School Improvement through Investors in People', *Educational Management and Administrative Journal of the British Educational Management and Administrative Society* 24(4): 371–79.

Brown, S. and Earley, P. (1990) *Enabling Teachers to Undertake INSET*, Slough: NFER.

Burrell, G. and Morgan, G. (1979) *Sociological Paradigms and Organisational Analysis: Elements of the Sociology of Corporate Life*, London: Heinemann.

Bush, T. and West-Burnham, J. (eds) (1994) *The Principles of Educational Management*, Harlow: Longman.

—— Bell, L., Bolam, R., Glatter, R. and Ribbins, P. (1999) *Redefining Educational Management: Policy, Practice and Research*, London: Falmer Press.

Caldwell, B.J. and Spinks, J.M. (1988) *The Self-Managing School*, Lewes: Falmer Press.

Capper, C. and Jamison, M. (1993) 'Let the Buyer Beware: Total Quality Management and Educational Research and Practice', *Educational Researcher* November: 25–30.

Carr, W. and Kemmis, S. (1986) *Becoming Critical: Education, Knowledge and Action Research*, Lewes: Falmer Press.

Cheeseman, C. (1997) 'Investors in People – the Re-Validation Experience', *Journal of the National Association for Staff Development* 36 (January): 35–7.

Coe, J. (1999) 'Learning Support Assistants', ongoing research, Oxford: Oxford Brookes University.

Cohen, L. and Manion, L. (1994 [1980]) *Research Methods in Education*, London: Routledge.

Collins, D., Jackson, M. and Bowen, J. (1996) 'Investors in People Review. Report 1', Hambledon Group; see also *Employee Development Bulletin* 77: 2.

Constable, J. and McCormack, R. (1987) *The Making of British Managers*, London: BIME–CBI.

Cordingley, P. (1999) 'The Teacher Training Agency's Research Agenda' in Bush et al.

Craft, A. (1996) *Continuing Professional Development: A Practical Guide for Teachers in Schools*, London: Routledge.

Creissen, T. and Ellison, L. (1996) 'Re-inventing School Leadership: Back to the Future in the UK?', paper presented at the Annual Meeting of the University Council for Educational Administration, Louisville, KY.

Dale, B. and Cooper, C. (1992) *Total Quality and Human Resources. An Executive Guide*, Oxford: Blackwell.

—— (1990) *Managing Primary Schools in the 1990s. A Professional Development Approach*, London: Paul Chapman.

—— (1993) *Foundations for Excellence*, Milton Keynes: Open University Press.

—— (1993) *Leadership and the Curriculum in the Primary School*, London: Paul Chapman.

—— Whittaker, P. and Wren, D. (1987), *Appraisal and Professional Development in the Primary School*, Milton Keynes: Open University Press.

Dean, J. (1991) 'Selling LEA Services', *Education Management Information Exchange*, Slough: NFER.

—— (1993) 'A Survey of the Organisation of LEA Inspection and Advisory Services', *Education Management Information Exchange*, Slough: NFER.

Debenham, T. (1996) 'Investors in People', *People Management*, 21 November.

Deming, W. Ewards (1982) *Out of the Crisis*, Cambridge: Cambridge University Press.

Department of Education (1993a) *The Government's Proposals for the Reform of Initial Teacher Training*, London: HMSO.

—— (1993b) *The Management and Provision of In-Service Training Funded by the Grant for Educational Support and Training*, London: HMSO.

—— OfSTED (1994) *Improving Schools*, London: HMSO.

Department for Education and Employment (1997a) *Excellence in Schools* (Cmnd 3681), London: HMSO.

—— (1997b) *The Standards Fund 1998/1999*, Circular 13/97, London: DfEE.

—— (1997c) *Initial Teacher Training*, Circular 10/97, London: DfEE.

—— (1997d) *Investors in People and School Improvement: Improving Schools Publication*, London: HMSO.

—— (1997e) *Teaching High Status, High Standards*, Circular 10/97, London: DfEE.

—— (1998a) *Teaching: High Status, High Standards: Requirements for Courses of Initial Teacher Training* Circular 4/98, London: HMSO.

—— (1998b) *Teachers Meeting the Challenge of Change*, Green Paper, London: HMSO.

—— (1999) *Teachers Meeting the Challenge of Change*, Technical Paper, London: HMSO.

—— (1999) *Pay and Performance Management*, Technical Paper, London: HMSO.

Department of Education and Science (1972) *Teacher Education and Training* (James Report), London: HMSO.

—— (1985) *Better Schools* (Cmnd 9469), London: HMSO.

—— (1988) *Education Reform Act*, London: HMSO.

—— (1989) *School Teacher Appraisal: A National Framework*, London: HMSO.

—— (1990) *Developing School Management: The Way Forward* (Report of the School Management Task Force), London: HMSO.

—— (1991a) *School Teacher Appraisal*, Circular 12/9, London: HMSO.

—— (1991b) *School-Based Initial Teacher Training in England and Wales*, London: HMSO.

—— (1992a) *Initial Teacher Training (Secondary Phase)*, Circular 9/92, London: HMSO.

—— (1992b) *Reform of Initial Teacher Training: A Consultation Document*, London: HMSO.

Doe, B. (1999) *ESRC Seminar Discussion*, 6–7 May, West Hill House, Birmingham.

Duignan and McPherson (1992) *Educative Leadership: A New Practical Theory for Administrators and Managers*, London: Falmer Press.

Earley, P. (1994) *Managing Our Greatest Resource: Evaluation of the Professional Development in Schools Project*, London: NFER.

—— Fidler, B. and Ouston, J. (eds) (1994) *Improvement through Inspection? Complementary Approaches to School Development*, London: David Fulton.

—— and Fletcher-Campbell, F. (1989) *The Time to Manage? Department and Faculty Heads at Work*, London: NFER–Nelson.

—— and Kinder, K. (1994) *Initiation Rites: Effective Induction Practices for New Teachers*, Slough: NFER.

—— (1999) 'School Governors', ongoing research, London: Institute of Education.

Egan (1994) in P. Earley, B. Fidler and J. Ouston (eds) *Improvement Through Inspection? Complementary Approaches to School Development*, London: David Fulton.

Elliot, J. (1996) 'School Effectiveness Research and its Critics', *Cambridge Journal of Education* 26: 199–224.

Everard, K.B. (1986) *Developing Management in Schools*, Oxford: Blackwell.

Foy, N. (1981) 'To Strengthen the Mixture, First Understand the Chemistry', *Guardian*, 2 September.

Fryer, R. (1997) 'We've Got to Get a Handle on Change', *Times Educational Supplement*, 28 November.

Fullan, M. (1985) 'Change Processes and Strategies at the Local Level', *Elementary School Journal* 85(3) 391–421.

—— (1991) 'The New Meaning in Educational Change' in P. Earley, B. Fidler, J. Ouston (eds) *Improvement Through Inspection? Complementary Approaches to School Development*, London: David Fulton.

—— and Hargreaves, A. (1992) *Understanding Teacher Development*, London: Cassell.

Furlong, J. (1994) 'Integration and Partnership in Initial Teacher Education – Dilemmas and Possibilities', in *Research Papers in Education* 9(3).

—— (1996) 'Do Student Teachers Need Higher Education?' in J. Furlong and R. Smith (eds) *The Role of Higher Education in Initial Teacher Training*, London: Kogan Page.

—— Hirst, P., Pocklington, K. and Miles, S. (1998) *Initial Teacher Training and the Role of the School*, Milton Keynes: Open University Press.

—— and Kane, I. (1996) 'Recognising Quality in Primary Initial Teacher Education', *UCET Occasional Paper No. 6.*, London: Universities Council for the Education of Teachers.

Further Education Funding Council (FEFC) (1993) *Assessing Achievement*, Circular 93\28, London: FEFC.

—— (1994) *Measuring Achievement*, Circular 94\31, London: FEFC.

—— (1997) *Learning Works, Widening Participation* (Kennedy Report), London: HMSO.

Gaunt, D. (1995) 'Supporting Continuing Professional Development' in H. Bines and J. Welton (eds) *Managing Partnership in Teacher Training and Development*, London: Routledge.

—— (1997) 'Building on the Past: New Opportunities for the Profession' in H. Tomlinson (ed.) *Managing Professional Development in Schools*, London: Paul Chapman.

General Teaching Council for England and Wales Trust (1993) *The Continuing Professional Development of Teachers*, London: GTC.

Glasser, W. (1990) 'The Quality School', *Phi Delta Kappa*, February: 425–36.

Gloucestershire Initial Teacher Education Partnership (1995) *Mentoring Handbook 1995–96*, Gloucester: Cheltenham and Gloucester College of Higher Education.

Gray, L. (1992) 'Foreword' to Edward Sallis and Peter Hingley, *Total Quality Management. Coombe Lodge Report 13(1)*, Bristol: Staff College, Blagdon.

Green, A. (1997) *Education, Globalisation and the Nation State*, Basingstoke: MacMillan.

Green, H. (1999) 'A View from the Teacher Training Agency's *Educational Management and Leadership ESRC Seminar* (7 May 1999)', London: TAA.

Green, K (1997) 'Managing Director of Qtab', *Management in People* 3 (6 February).

211

Greenfield, T. and Ribbins, P. (1993) *Greenfield on Educational Administration: Towards a Humane Science*, London: Routledge.

Guest D.E. (1989) 'Personnel and HRM: Can You Tell the Difference?', *Personnel Management* 21(1): 48–51.

Hall, A. (1999) 'Green Paper is Good News for Good Staff', *Times Educational Supplement*, 29 January.

Hall, V. and Oldroyd, D. (1990a) *Management Self-development for Staff in Secondary Schools* , Unit 1: *Self-development for Effective Management*, Bristol: NDCEMP.

—— (1990b) *Management Self-development for Staff in Secondary Schools*, Unit 2: *Policy, Planning and Change*, Bristol: NDCEMP.

—— (1990c) *Management Self-development for Staff in Secondary Schools*, Unit 3: *Team Development for Effective Schools*, Bristol: NDCEMP.

—— (1990d) *Management Self-development for Staff in Secondary Schools*, Unit 4: *Implementing and Evaluating*, Bristol: NDCEMP.

Handy, C. (1993) *Understanding Organisations* (4th edn), Harmondsworth: Penguin.

—— and Aitken, R. (1986) *Understanding Schools as Organisations*, Harmondsworth: Penguin.

Hargreaves, A. and Fullan, M. (1992) *What's Worth Fighting For in Your School?*, Milton Keynes : Open University Press.

Hargreaves, D. H. (1995) 'Self-Managing Schools and Development Planning – Chaos or Control?', *School Organisation* 15(3): 215–17.

—— (1996) 'Teaching as a Research-Based Profession: Possibilities and Prospects', TTA Annual Lecture, London: TTA.

Harrison, B.T. (1995) 'Re-evaluating Leadership and Service in Educational Management' in J. Bell and B.T. Harrison (eds) *Vision and Values in Managing Education*, London: David Fulton.

Hart, C. (1998) 'Investors in People: A Case Study', MA thesis, Oxford: Oxford Brookes University.

Hillage, J. and Moralee, J. (1996) 'The Return of Investors', *Institute of Employment Studies*; see also *Employee Development Bulletin* 82: 2.

Hitchcock, G. and Hughes, D. (1989) *Research and the Teacher: A Qualitative Introduction to School-Based Research*, London: Routledge.

Hixon, J. and Lovelace, K. (1993) 'Total Quality Management's Challenge to Urban Schools', *Educational Leadership* 50(3): 24–7.

HMI (1998) 'Extract from the Annual Report of Her Majesty's Chief Inspector of Schools 1996 – 97', *HEADLAMP*, paras 292–94, London: HMI.

Holmes, G. (1993) *Essential School Leadership*, London: Kogan Page.

Holt, M. (1993) 'The Educational Consequences of W. Edwards Deming', *Phi Delta Kappa* January: 382–88.

Honey, P. and Mumford, A. (1982) *The Manual of Learning Styles*, Maidenhead: Peter Honey.

Hutton, W. (1995) *The State We're In*, London: Jonathan Cape.

Investors in People UK (1996) *Investors in People: the Revised Indicators – Advice and Guidance for Practitioners*, London: IIP.

Issac, J. (1995) 'Self-Management and Development' in J. Bell and B.T. Harrison (eds) *Vision and Values in Managing Education*, London: David Fulton.

Johnson, D. (1984) 'Planning Small-Scale Research' in T. Bell, A. Bush, J. Fox, J. Goddley and S. Goulding (eds) *Conducting Small-Scale Investigations in Educational Management*, London: Paul Chapman.

Joyce, B. and Showers, B. (1980) 'The Coaching of Teaching', *Educational Leadership* 40: 4–10.

Juran, J. (1989) *Juran on Leadership for Quality*, New York: MacMillan.

Keenoy, T. (1990) 'HRM: A Case of the Wolf in Sheep's Clothing', *Personnel Review* 19(2): 3–9.

Langtree Training and Conference Centre (1997) *Investors in People*, Wigan: Langtree Training and Conference Centre Ltd.

Lawton, D. (1993) 'Political Parties, Ideology and the National Curriculum', *Educational Review* 45(2): 111–18.

Lee, M. (1997) 'The Development of In-Service Education and Training as Seen through the Pages of the *British Journal of In-Service Education*', *British Journal of In-Service Education* 23(1).

Lee, R. (1996) 'The "Pay-Forward" View of Training', *People Management* 2 (8 February).

Legge, K. (1989) 'HRM: a Critical Analysis' in J. Storey (ed.) *New Perspectives on Human Resource Management*, London: Routledge.

Leuenberger, J.A., Whitaker, J. and Sheldon, V., Jr (1993) *The Total Quality Movement in Education*, Commonwealth Foundation and the University Press of America, PA.

Levacic, R. and Glover, D. (1995) *OfSTED Assessment of Schools' Efficiency*, Milton Keynes: Open University Press (EPAM Report).

Lieberman, A. (1986), *Rethinking School Improvement: Research, Craft and Concept*, Columbia, OH: Teachers' College Press.

Lloyd, C. and Rawlinson, M. (1992) 'New Technology and Human Resource Management' in P. Blyton and P. Turnbull (eds) *Reassessing Human Resource Management*, London: Sage.

London Borough of Hounslow LEA (1986) *Management Training Scheme*, London: Hounslow LEA.

Madden, C. and Mitchell, V. (1993) *Professions, Standards and Competence: A Survey of Continuing Education for the Professions*, University of Bristol: Department for Continuing Education.

McIntyre, D., Hagger, H. and Wilkin, M. (eds) (1993) *Mentoring: Perspectives on School-Based Teacher Education*, London: Kogan Page.

McKinnon, D., Statham, J. and Hales, M. (1996) *Education in the UK: Facts and Figures*, Milton Keynes: Open University Press.

McMahon, A. (1999) 'Educational Leadership, Administration and Management', paper presented at the *ESRC Seminar*, 6–7 May, West Hill House, Birmingham.

McNamara, D. (1996) 'The University, the Academic Tradition and Education', in J. Furlong and R. Smith (eds) *The Role of Higher Education in Initial Teacher Training*, London: Kogan Page.

Male, T. (1997) 'A Critical Review of Headteacher Professional Development in England and Wales', paper presented at the *Annual Meeting of the American Educational Research Association*, Chicago, IL.

Manchester LEA (1986) *Model for Self-Evaluation*, Manchester: Manchester LEA.

Mannix, P. (1998) 'Superteacher, Supersceptics', *The Teacher*, April.

Marsh, J. (1991) 'Different Approaches', *Managing Service Quality*, Bristol: Avon TEC.

Merton, R.K. and Kendall, P.L. (1946) 'The Focused Interview', *American Journal of Sociology* 51: 541–57.

Millett, A. (1995) 'Securing Excellence in Teaching', Teacher Training Agency *First Annual Lecture*, London: TTA.

—— (1996a) 'Teacher Researchers', Introduction to D.H. Hargreaves 'Teaching as a Research-Based Profession', *TTA Annual Lecture*, London: TTA.

—— (1996b) 'Chief Executive's Speech: TTA's Corporate Plan, 1996–97', *TTA Annual General Meeting*, London: TTA.

—— (1998) 'Chief Executive's Speech, 1997–98', *TTA Annual General Meeting*, London: TTA.

Mills, A.R. and Murgatroyd, S. (1991) *Organisational Rules – A Framework for Understanding Organisational Action*, Milton Keynes: Open University Press.

MORI (1995) *Survey of Continuing Professional Development*, London: MORI.

Mortimore, P., Sammon, P., Stoll, L., Lewis, D. and Ecob, R. (1988) *School Matters: the Junior Years*, Salisbury: Open Books.

Mumford, A. (1989) *Management Development: Strategies for Action*, London: Institute of Personnel Management.

—— (1997) *How Managers Can Develop Managers*, Aldershot: Gower.

Murgatroyd, S. (1991) 'Strategy Structure and Quality Service: Developing School-Wide Quality Improvement', *School Organisation* 11(1): 7–14.

—— and Morgan, C. (1993) *Total Quality Management and the School*, Buckingham: Open University Press.

Myer, M.W. and Zucker, L.G. (1989) *Permanently Failing Organisations*, Beverly Hills, CA: Sage.

NACETT (1996) *Skills for 2000: Report on Progress towards the National Targets for Education and Training*, London: National Advisory Council for Education and Training.

National Advisory Group for Continuing Education and Lifelong Learning (NAGCELL) (1997) *Lifelong Learning*, London: HMSO.

National Committee of Inquiry into Higher Education (1997) *Higher Education in the Learning Society*, (the Dearing Review), London: HMSO.

National Educational Assessment Centre (NEAC) (1996) *Annual Report 1995–96*, Oxford: NEAC.

—— (1999) *Development Programme for Middle Managers*, Oxford: NEAC–Oxford Brookes University.

National Foundation for Educational Research (NFER) (1990) *Enabling Teachers to Undertake IN-SERVICE Education and Training: A Report to the DES*, Slough: NFER.

National Policy Board for Education Administration (NPBEA) (1993), *Principles for Our Changing Schools*, Virginia: NPBEA.

National Steering Group (NSG) (1991) *School Teacher Appraisal: A National Framework*, London: HMSO.

National Union of Teachers (NUT) (1993a) *Appraisal*, London: NUT.

—— (1993b) *Information and Guidance for Headteachers and Deputy Headteachers*, London: NUT.

Oakland, J. (1989) *Total Quality Management*, London: Butterworth.

Office for Standards in Education (OfSTED) (1993) *The Management and Provision of In-service Training Funded by GEST*, London: HMSO.
—— (1994) *Improving Schools*, London: HMSO.
—— (1996) 'In-Service Training. Key Issues for Schools' in *Subjects and Standards: Issues for School Development arising from OfSTED Inspections, Findings 94–95, Key Stages 3 and 4*, London: HMSO.
—— (1997) *Nursery and Primary School Inspection Schedule*, London: HMSO.
—— (1998) *Making Headway*, London: OfSTED.
—— (1999) News Release 99–22, 25 May 1999.
Oldroyd, D. and Hall, V. (1991) *Managing Staff Development: A Handbook for Secondary Schools*, London: Paul Chapman Publishing.
Ogbonna, E. (1992) 'Organisational Culture and Human Resource Management: Dilemmas and Contradictions' in P. Blyton and P. Turnbull (eds), *Reassessing Human Resource Management*, London: Sage.
Ormston, M. (1996) *Leadership and Leadership Qualities*, Oxford: School of Education, Oxford Brookes University.
—— and Shaw, M. (1993) *Mentoring*, Oxford: School of Education, Oxford Brookes University.
Ott, J.S. (1989) *The Organisational Perspective*, Pacific Grove, CA: Brooks-Cole.
Owens, R. and Shakeshaft, K. (1992) 'The New Revolution in Administrative Theory', *Journal of Educational Administration* 30(2): 4–16.
Oxford Brookes University (1998) *Mentors 1998–1999*, Oxford: School of Education, Oxford Brookes University.
—— (1999) *Career Entry Profile: Notes for Tutors*, Oxford: School of Education, Oxford Brookes University.
Paine, J., Turner, P. and Pryke, R. (1992) *Total Quality in Education*, Sydney: Ashton.
Parker, G. (1994) *Headteachers' Leadership and Management Programme – Consultation*, London: TTA.
—— (1995) *The Continuing Professional Development of Teachers*, London: TTA.
Peters, T. (1987) *Thriving on Chaos*, London: Pan Books.
Pfeffer and Coote (1991) *Success Against the Odds*, London: Routledge .
Phillips, E. and Pugh, D. S. (1988) *How to Get a PhD: Managing the Peaks and Troughs of Research*, Milton Keynes: Open University Press.
Philips, J. (1999) 'Green Paper', *Times Educational Supplement* 19 March.
—— (1999) 'Back to the Drawing Board', *Times Educational Supplement* 19 March.
—— (1999) 'Not Learning but Coasting', *Times Educational Supplement* 24 March.
Pickard, J. (1996) 'Investors in People', *People Management* 21 (November).
Poole, M. (1990) 'Editorial: HRM – an International Perspective', *International Journal of Human Resource Management* 1(1): 1–11.
Poulson, Louise (1996) 'Accountability: A key Word in the Discourse of Educational Reform', *Journal of Educational Policy* 11(5): 579–92.
Pring, R. (1996) 'Just Desert' in J. Furlong and R. Smith (eds) *The Role of Higher Education in Initial Teacher Training*, London: Kogan Page.
—— (1998) 'Universities and Teacher Education', paper presented at the *Annual Conference of the Standing Conference on Studies in Education*, November.
Pugh, D.S. and Hickson, D. J. (1989) *Writers on Organisations* (4th edn), Harmondsworth: Penguin.

Purkey, S. and Smith, M. (1983) 'Effective Schools: a Review', *The Elementary School Journal* 83(4): 427–52.

Quong, T. and Walker, A. (1996) 'TQM and School Restructuring: a Case Study', *School Organisation* 16(2): 219–31.

Rawlings, J. (1997) 'The Role of the Staff Development Coordinator in Schools', MA management paper, Oxford: Oxford Brookes University.

Riches, C. and Morgan, C. (1989) *Human Resource Management in Education*, Milton Keynes: Open University Press.

Rix, A., Parkinson, R. and Gaunt, R. (1994) *Investors in People: A Qualitative Study of Employers*, Employment Department Research Series Report No. 21, London: HMSO.

Rosenholtz, S. J. (1989) *Teachers' Workplace: the Social Organisation of Schools*, New York: Longman.

—— Basster, O. and Hoover Dempsey, K. (1986), 'Organisational Conditions of Teacher Learning', *Teaching and Teacher Education* 2(2).

Roth, R. (ed.) (1999) 'University as Context for Teacher Development' in *The Role of the University in the Preparation of Teachers*, London: Falmer Press.

Rutter, M., Maugham, B., Mortimore, P. and Ouston, J. (1979) *Fifteen Thousand Hours*, London: Open Books.

Sammons, P., Hillman, J. and Mortimer, P. (1995) *Key Characteristics of Effective Schools: A Review of Effectiveness Research*, London: OfSTED.

Sallis, E. (1993) *Total Quality Management in Education*, London: Kogan Page.

—— (1996) 'Linking Quality and Financial Management: a College Case Study', *Developing Quality Schools* 1(3), Ontario Institute for Studies in Education.

Sapsford, R. J. and Evans, J. (1984) 'Evaluating a Research Report' in J. Bell, T. Bush, A. Fox, J. Goodley and S. Goulding (eds) (1984) *Conducting Small-Scale Investigations in Educational Management*, London: Paul Chapman.

Schein, S. (1984) *Organisation Culture and Leadership*, Oxford: Blackwell

—— (1992) 'Coming to a New Awareness of Organisational Culture' in G. Salaman, S. Cameron, H. Hamblin, P. Lles, C. Mabey and K. Thompson (eds) *Human Resource Strategies*, London: Sage Publications.

Schmoker, M. and Wilson, R. (1993) *Total Quality Education*, Bloomington, IN: Phi Delta Kappa.

Schon, D.A. (1987) *Educating the Reflective Practitioner*, London: Josey-Bass.

School Management Task Force (1990) *Developing School Management: the Way Forward*, London: HMSO.

Sebba, J. (1999) 'A View from the Standards and Effectiveness Unit', paper presented at the *Redefining Educational Management and Leadership ESRC Seminar*, 7 May, London: DfEE.

Senge, P.M. (1990) *The Fifth Discipline – The Art and Practice of the Learning Organisation*, New York: Doubleday.

Sevick, C. (1993) 'Can Deming's Concept of Total Quality Management be Applied to Education?' paper presented to the *Annual Conference on Creating Quality Schools*, March, Oklahoma City.

Sergiovanni, T.J. (1992) 'Why We Should Ask Substitutes for Leadership', *Educational Leadership* 49(5): 41–5.

Shaw, M., Boydell, D. and Warner, F. (1995) 'Developing Induction in Schools: Managing the Transition from Training to Employment' in H. Bines and J.

Welton (eds) *Managing Partnership in Teacher Training and Development*, London: Routledge.

Slater, J. (1999) 'Extra Year to Spot the Future Failure', *Times Educational Supplement*, 19 March.

Spinks (1990) 'Collaborative Decision-making at the School Level' in J. Chapman (ed.) *School-Based Decision-Making and Management*, Basingstoke: Falmer Press.

Spooner, B. (1999) 'Green for Danger', *The Teacher*, April.

Squire, L. and Blandford, S. (1997) 'The Impact of the Headteacher Leadership and Management Programme (HEADLAMP) on LEA Induction and Management Development Provision for New Headteachers', paper presented at the *Annual General Meeting of the British Educational Management and Administration Society*, Cambridge, England.

Statutory Instruments (1999) *Education, England and Wales: the Education (Induction Arrangements for School Teachers) (England) Regulations 1999*, No. 1065, London: HMSO.

Stoll, L. and Fink, D. (1992) 'Effecting School Change: the Halton Approach', *School Effectiveness and School Improvement* 3(92).

—— (1996) *Changing Our Schools*, Bullyhan: Open University Press.

Storey, J. (1987) 'Developments in the Management of Human Resources; an Interim Report', *Warwick Papers in Industrial Relations No. 17*, Warwick: IRRU, School of Industrial and Business Studies, University of Warwick.

—— (1992) *Developments in the Management of Human Resources*, Oxford: Blackwell.

Straker, H. (1998) 'Turn On the New Life Support System', *Times Educational Supplement*, 22 May.

Sutcliffe, J. (1999) 'Put a Tiger in Your GTC', *Times Educational Supplement*, 21 May.

Taylor, W. (1994) 'Quality Assurance' in M. Wilkin and D. Sankey, (eds) *Collaboration and Transition in Initial Teacher Training*, London: Kogan Page.

Teacher Training Agency (TTA) (1994) Inaugural Conference Programme, London: TTA.

—— (1995) *Initial Advice to the Secretary of State on the Continuing Professional Development of Teachers*, London: TTA.

—— (1996a) 'National Standards for Teachers', *TTA News*, November.

—— (1996b) *Effective Training though Partnership: Working Papers on Secondary Partnership*, London: TTA.

—— (1997) *Effective Training though Partnership: Working Papers on Primary Partnership*, London: TTA.

—— (1998a) *Requirements for All Courses of Initial Teacher Training* (Annex 1 of DfEE Circular 4/98), London: TTA.

—— (1998b) *Report on the Outcomes of the NPQH Trials 1996–97*, London: TTA.

—— (1998c) *Standards for the Award of Qualified Teacher Status* (Annex A of DfEE Circular 4/98), London: TTA.

—— (1998d) *Leadership Programme for Serving Headteachers. Information and Application*, London: TTA.

—— (1998e) *National Standards for Teachers*, London: TTA.

—— (1999a) *Career Entry Profile: Notes of Guidelines and Standards 1999*, London: TTA.

—— (1999b) *Career Entry Profile*, Letter to Teacher Education Institutions, 4 February.

—— (1999c) *Career Entry Profile for NQTs*, London: TTA.

Terry, P.M. (1996) 'Using Total Quality Management Principles to Implement School-Based Management', paper presented at the *Annual International Conference of the International Association of Management*, Toronto, Canada.

(The) Teacher (1999) 'Comment: "It May Be Green But Is It Good for You?" ', *The Teacher*, February.

TES (1994) 'Flying High with the Kitemark', 11 February.

Thomas, P. (1996) 'A Comprehensive School's Experience of Working Towards Investors in People' in P. Earley, B. Fidler and J. Ouston (eds) *Improvement through Inspection? Complementary Approaches to School Development,* London: David Fulton.

Thompson, M. (1999) 'A View from a Teachers' Association', paper presented at the *Redefining Educational Management and Leadership ESRC Seminar*, 7 May, London: Association of Teachers and Lecturers.

Tomlinson, H. (1993) 'Developing Professionals', *Education* 24 (September).

—— (ed.) (1997) 'Continuing Professional Development in the Professions' in *Managing Professional Development in Schools*, London: Paul Chapman.

Tomlinson, J. (1993) *The Control of Education*, London: Cassell.

Tooley, J. and Darby, J. (1998) *Educational Research*, London: OfSTED.

Tuckman, B.W. (1972) *Conducting Educational Research*, New York: Harcourt Brace Jovanovich.

Wallace, M. (1989) 'Towards a Collegiate Approach to Curriculum Management in Primary and Middle Schools' in M. Preedy (ed.) *Approaches to Curriculum Management*, Milton Keynes: Open University Press.

Warwick, D. (1983) *Decision Making*, London: The Industrial Society.

Watkins, J. and Drury, L. (1994) *Positioning for the Unknown: Career Development for Professions in the 1990s*, Bristol: University of Bristol.

West-Burnham, J. (1994) 'Strategy, Policy and Planning' in T. Bush and J. West-Burnham (eds) *The Principles of Educational Management*, Harlow: Longman.

Wilkin, M. (1999) 'The Role of Higher Education in Initial Teacher Education', *Universities Council for Educating Teachers*, Occasional Paper No 12, London: UCET.

Williams, M. (1993) 'Changing Policies and Practices' in *The Continuing Professional Development of Teachers*, London: General Teaching Council for England and Wales.

Williams, T. and Green, A. (1997) *Business Approach to Training*, London: Gower.

Zienau, N. (1996) 'Investors in People: A Consultant's View' in P. Earley, B. Fidler and J. Ouston (eds) *Improvement through Inspection? Complementary Approaches to School Development*, London: David Fulton.

INDEX

Boldface denotes references of major importance